TWAYNE'S WORLD AUTHORS SERIES
A Survey of the World's Literature

CANADA

Robert Lecker, University of Maine

EDITOR

Brian Moore

TWAS 632

Brian Moore

Photo credit: Betty Dahlie

BRIAN MOORE

By HALLVARD DAHLIE
University of Calgary

TWAYNE PUBLISHERS
A DIVISION OF G. K. HALL & CO., BOSTON

Published in 1981 by Twayne Publishers,
A Division of G. K. Hall & Co.
All Rights Reserved

Printed on permanent/durable acid-free paper and bound
in the United States of America

First Printing

Library of Congress Cataloging in Publication Data

Dahlie, Hallvard.
Brian Moore.

(Twayne's world authors series ; TWAS 632 : Canada)
Bibliography: p. 158-65
Includes index.
1.   Moore, Brian, 1921-   —Criticism and interpretation.
PR9199.3.M617Z63   1981   813'.54   80-27502
ISBN 0-8057-6475-5

To Betty

Contents

About the Author

Hallvard Dahlie, professor of English at the University of Calgary, was born in Norway and came to Canada at an early age, receiving his elementary and secondary education in Alberta and British Columbia. He earned his B.A. and M.A. at the University of British Columbia, and his Ph.D. at the University of Washington. He taught high school in British Columbia for many years, and has been at the University of Calgary since 1967, where he also served as head of the English Department for five years. Dr. Dahlie has published an earlier monograph on Brian Moore, as well as articles on such other Canadian writers as Malcolm Lowry, Frederick Philip Grove, Alice Munro, and Morley Callaghan.

Preface

In this study I examine the components of Brian Moore's work roughly in chronological order, as he moves from his early Belfast preoccupations to the larger North American and world scenes. I am concerned mainly with his eleven novels, but since they have up to this point been neglected, I also give some attention to his other writings—his excellent short stories, his literary criticism, and his nonfiction prose, particularly his documentary novel, *The Revolution Script*. It has been my experience that what Moore has to say in these varied writings is not only intrinsically interesting, but adds significantly to our understanding of both his moral vision and his fictional processes.

It soon becomes evident in this study what avid Moore readers have always known, that the uniqueness and delight of his fiction derive in part from the way it regularly defies our expectations. One of the difficulties, therefore, that I encountered in organizing my approach was the establishing of viable groupings of his novels, for a number of equally workable possibilities presented themselves. And of course the fact that Moore is still creating more fiction as I write this[1] might well render my chapter titles even more tenuous, although, with any luck, perhaps not my observations and conclusions about his stature as a novelist.

This study constitutes for the moment a culmination of my interest in Moore, which began when I heard him read from his then soon-to-be-published *Answer from Limbo* at the Vancouver Public Library in 1962, and which led to my Doctoral dissertation at the University of Washington. It is an expansion of my earlier Copp Clark and now out-of-print monograph that covered his first six novels, much of which, with the kind permission of Douglas & McIntyre, I have freely adapted here. I also wish to thank the editors of *Critique: Studies in Modern Fiction, Canadian Literature*, and *Ploughshares* for permission to use material originally published in those journals, and Mr. Brian Moore, Mr. Hugh MacLennan, and Mr. Edward Weeks for permission to quote from their letters housed in the *Brian Moore Collection*.

My preparation of this manuscript at the University of Calgary has been greatly facilitated by its library resources and by the cooperation of the Director of Libraries, Mr. Alan H. MacDonald, and his staff. I wish in this respect to express my appreciation for permission to use the material in the *Brian Moore Collection*, University of Calgary Library, Special Collections Division; particular thanks must go to the Special Collections Librarian, Apollonia Steele, and the University Archivist, Jean Tener, who, along with members of their staff, very much facilitated my examination of material from this *Collection*. I am indebted to the University of Calgary for the granting of a sabbatical leave to undertake this study, and for a research grant to help me complete it. I am grateful, too, to the Department of English for making its resources available to me during the year, and I particularly wish to thank Mrs. Betty O'Keeffe for her superb work in typing and proofreading my manuscript.

There remain three individuals who have shared very much in this work. Brian and Jean Moore's gracious friendship and hospitality over the years have helped make this study a genuine pleasure to undertake; Moore's comments on his own work and responses to my many queries have always been most generously given, and have very much helped me keep things in perspective. Finally, I owe a special thanks to my wife, Betty, who in the midst of her own career has steadily supported and encouraged my work, and whose sensitive reading of Moore's works has richly complemented my own interpretations.

HALLVARD DAHLIE

University of Calgary

Chronology

1921   Born August 25, second son and fourth child, to James Bernard Moore and Eileen (McFadden) Moore.

1927-   Attended Newington Elementary School and Saint Mala-
1938   chy's College, Belfast.

1938-   Enrolled in University of London courses in Belfast.
1939

1940-   Service in Belfast Air Raid Precautions Unit and National
1942   Fire Service.

1943   Joined British Ministry of War Transport and saw service in North Africa.

1943-   Accompanied Allied occupation forces as port official into
1945   Italy and southern France. Worked in ports of Naples and Marseilles.

1945-   Served with UNRRA Economic Mission in Warsaw and as
1947   a free-lance reporter in Scandinavia. Returned to England at end of 1947.

1948   Emigrated to Canada; worked as clerk in construction camp at Thessalon, Ontario, from February to November 1948.

1949-   Worked as proofreader (six months) and then as reporter
1955   for the *Montreal Gazette;* published several pulp stories in *Weekend Magazine.*

1951   Married first wife, Jacqueline (Scully) Sirois. Publication of first serious short story, "Sassenach." Publication of first two pulp novels, *The Executioners* and *Wreath for a Redhead.*

1953   Became Canadian citizen.

1954   Birth of son. Publication of *French for Murder* under pseudonym Bernard Mara.

1955   *Judith Hearne; A Bullet for My Lady* under pseudonym Bernard Mara. Won Beta Sigma Phi Award and Authors' Club of Great Britain Annual First Novel Award for *Judith Hearne.*

1956   *This Gun for Gloria* under pseudonym Bernard Mara; *Intent to Kill* under pseudonym Michael Bryan.

1957   *The Feast of Lupercal; Murder in Majorca* under pseudonym Michael Bryan.

1958   Invited to Yaddo as guest writer by Granville Hicks. Won Quebec Literary Prize for *The Feast of Lupercal.*

1959   Received Guggenheim Fellowship. Moved to Amagansett, Long Island, and New York.
1960   Publication of *The Luck of Ginger Coffey*. Received Governor-General's Award for Fiction.
1961   Worked with Daniel Petrie and Jose Quintano (Directors) on stage version of *Judith Hearne*. Won Canada Council Award to go to London to write new novel. Received National Institute of Arts and Letters Grant.
1962   *An Answer from Limbo*.
1963   *Canada* (with Editors of *Life*). *The Luck of Ginger Coffey* presented as an opera at the O'Keefe Centre in Toronto.
1964   Wrote film script for *Ginger Coffey*.
1965   Moved to California to write *Torn Curtain* for Alfred Hitchcock. *The Emperor of Ice-Cream*.
1967   Married second wife, Jean Denney.
1968   *I Am Mary Dunne*.
1969   *Brian Moore* by Hallvard Dahlie.
1970   *Fergus*.
1971   *The Revolution Script*.
1972   *Catholics*.
1973   Won W. H. Smith Literary Award for *Catholics*.
1973-   Adjunct Professor at UCLA.
1980
1974   Appointed Regents' Professor UCLA. *Brian Moore* by Jeanne Flood.
1975   *The Great Victorian Collection*. Received Governor-General's Award for Fiction. Won James Tait Black Memorial Award. Moore papers and manuscripts deposited with University of Calgary.
1976   *The Doctor's Wife*. Fellow of the Royal Society of Literature (England).
1977   Production of *Emperor of Ice-Cream* by Abbey Theatre in Dublin.
1977-   Serious illness in Dublin and Los Angeles.
1978
1978   *Two Stories*.
1979   *The Mangan Inheritance*.
1980   March, BBC program "Writers and Places" devoted to Brian Moore and his works.
1981   *The Temptations of Eileen Hughes*.

CHAPTER 1

The Shaping of a Career

ALONG with Malcolm Lowry, Brian Moore has been aptly labeled by George Woodcock as one of those "splendid birds of passage" who from time to time set down on Canadian soil, write a novel or two, and then take flight again. Certainly the record of Moore's life supports this analogy, and it may ultimately be impossible to decide whether he rightfully belongs to his country of birth, Northern Ireland, his country of citizenship, Canada, or his normal country of domicile, the United States. All three of these nations have on occasion claimed him, ignored him, or rejected him, but it is clear that the cultures and societies of all three play significant roles in his fiction.

At the moment, however, Irish situations and characters have a clear edge: only in *I Am Mary Dunne* (1968), *The Revolution Script* (1971), and *The Great Victorian Collection* (1975) are these elements absent. North American components are juxtaposed against their Irish counterparts in *The Luck of Ginger Coffey* (1960), *An Answer from Limbo* (1962), *Fergus* (1970), *The Doctor's Wife* (1976), and *The Mangan Inheritance* (1979), while the four remaining novels, *Judith Hearne* (1955), *The Feast of Lupercal* (1957), *The Emperor of Ice-Cream* (1965), and *Catholics* (1972), exploit exclusively various elements of the Irish scene. And the two full-length critical studies of Moore to date essentially perpetuate the national ambiguity that attends him: my own 1969 monograph was published as one of the Studies in Canadian Literature Series, while Jeanne Flood's 1974 book was a contribution to the Irish Writers Series.

It is not surprising, therefore, that questions persist about his national status, until it seems at times that only Moore himself is unconcerned about it, a point he whimsically discussed in an interview over a decade ago:

It's almost as though fate had cast me in the perfect role of the outsider without my even being aware of it. It starts with this: [though I am a

Catholic] I have a Protestant name, and I come from the North of Ireland. Therefore, when I wrote a book about Catholics, all the Catholics tended to discount it, because they thought it was written by a Protestant. Then, when . . . someone in Ireland might have started writing about me, it was announced that I was living in Canada and was really a Canadian who was pretending to write Irish novels. I embraced the Canadians with both arms and became a Canadian citizen and announced to everyone that I was a Canadian writer, whereupon I spent my life being told by Canadians that I'm not really a Canadian. . . . When I had lived in New York for several years, I don't think I met an American publisher or writer who didn't still believe I lived in Montreal, and I'm sure that nobody knows where I'm living now except you![1]

There is no doubt that this confusion still exists in the minds of many readers, but Moore's status today as a Canadian novelist derives quite simply from two tangible facts: his long-held Canadian citizenship and his own frequently expressed desire to be called a Canadian writer. All readers, however, would agree that this issue is ultimately not as important as the multiplicity and complexity of his fictional worlds, and the artistry with which Moore reflects these worlds.

In aesthetic terms, too, Moore is in an enigmatic position; he at once both denies the usual fictional categories and embraces them all: he has been variously classified as a Realist, a Naturalist, an Existentialist, a comic writer, an exile writer, a Catholic writer, and an anti-Catholic writer. He is not a "popular" writer in the sense of making the best-seller lists, but his fiction has had a wide readership throughout the world, both in English and in translation, and his works are seriously studied by academics and students on both sides of the Atlantic. Two of his novels have been turned into successful films, and he has won numerous awards for his fiction, including the James Tait Memorial Award and W. H. Smith Award in Britain, a Guggenheim Fellowship in the United States, and two Governor-General's Awards in Canada.

All this bespeaks a wide and respectable reputation for Moore, but he has assiduously avoided the literary limelight, and in his private life, too, he is essentially a loner. He has developed his artistry and formulated his vision quite independently of any of the literary groups which have from time to time been dominant on both sides of the Atlantic, though he quite readily concedes a literary debt in particular to James Joyce, but also to Flaubert, Dostoevsky, and more recently, to Jorge Luis Borges. But whatever tradition or nation we look at, Moore remains essentially removed from the standard literary groups of all three nations; in a very real sense, the only category that fits is the one he has on many occasions proclaimed for himself—the writer as exile—a designation which the facts of his life and career seem fully to support.

I *Life and Career*

Brian Moore[2] was born in Belfast, Northern Ireland, on August 25, 1921, one of nine children of the late James Bernard and Eileen (McFadden) Moore. He grew up in a close and strict family atmosphere, where both parents were uncompromisingly honest, and for whom family, education, and religion were without question accepted as the major forces that give meaning and direction to one's life. His father, largely self-educated, became a prominent surgeon and university lecturer in Belfast, and was, as Moore recalls, a man "who couldn't understand failure of any kind." The Moore family had originally been Protestant, but Brian's grandfather, a Belfast lawyer, had converted late in his life to Catholicism, and the young Moore was thus brought up under the doctrines of that faith, though he early rebelled against all forms of institutionalized religion. He attended various Catholic schools in Belfast, including Saint Malachy's College, which he left in 1938 without graduating, and though he later registered for courses offered by the University of London, the outbreak of World War II effectively terminated his formal education.

The decade of the 1940s was for Moore a crucial one in the shaping of his eventual career as an exile and a writer, for the events of that period catapulted him suddenly from a parochial backwater into the course of history, as it were. As a youthful volunteer in Belfast's Air Raid Precautions Unit and National Fire Service, he experienced the German blitzes on that city which began in April of 1941; he accompanied the Allied Occupation Forces into North Africa, France, and Italy as a port officer with the British Ministry of War Transport; he saw the death camps at Auschwitz and the Russian armies advancing across Poland; as an official with the UNRRA Economic Mission, he participated in the reconstruction of Warsaw; and he traveled through Finland, Sweden, Norway, and Denmark as a free-lance journalist, recording his observations and impressions of a world that was far removed from the closed world of Belfast.

But dramatic as they were, all these events in Europe were not sufficient to hold him in the Old World. "In Europe I had been a spectator at events which were not *my* events," he recounted many years later,[3] and his subsequent decision to emigrate to Canada, his marriage to a Canadian, and his assumption of Canadian citizenship all reflected the decisiveness of his break from the Old World and his anticipation of New World possibilities; both his life and his fiction, however, make it clear that this transition has not always been a comfortable or easy one. In a literal sense he has lived a relatively uprooted existence even after coming to North America: his moving from Thessalon to Toronto to Montreal, from Long Island to New York to Malibu, his frequent travels to Canada, Ireland, and Europe, all bespeak an active exile indeed. Yet his happy domestic life with his second wife (the former Jean Denney of Kentville, Nova Scotia), his teaching responsibilities with UCLA, and his strictly disciplined daily routine of physical exercise, research, and writing all reflect a man very much rooted in the realities and stabilities of life.

Moore's commitment to a career of writing has been serious, one he has pursued literally in sickness and in health: at an early stage of *Judith Hearne* he suffered a serious concussion in a boating accident in the Laurentians, and more recently he persevered with *The Mangan Inheritance* through a prolonged critical illness in Dublin and Los Angeles. His "Work and Publishing Diaries," now lodged in the Special Collections Division of the University of Calgary, record meticulously the details of how his short stories and novels grow from original impulse to final draft, and his correspondence with literary agents, publishers, and critics displays not only a generous courtesy but an intelligent grasp of the whole fictional process. His literary output over the past three decades has been steady and quite exceptional: aside from his substantial pulp fiction (some seven novels, and about twenty stories), he has published a dozen quality short stories, eleven novels, a documentary novel on the FLQ crisis, a book on Canada for the Time-Life series, close to fifty articles and reviews, numerous stage and screen versions of his own novels,as well as film scripts for such Hollywood notables as the late Sir Alfred Hitchcock.

II   *Influences on His Writing*

In an oversimplified sense, Moore has become a novelist in spite of his family, his religion, and his education, the three normal formative influences of youth, for from them he received virtually no direct encouragement to pursue a writing career. Not surprisingly, however, their indirect influences are there, for out of these three forces arise many of the recurring tensions in his fiction, where frequently the central conflicts can be seen as dramatizations of the issues which very much shaped Moore's own responses to his world. Though early in his life he rejected the narrow, institutionalized dogma of his parents, his admiration for individuals who subscribe to a strong faith is reflected in such fictional portraits as Professor O'Neill in *Judith Hearne*, Eileen Tierney in *An Answer from Limbo*, and the ghosts of Mr. and Mrs. Fadden in *Fergus*. "He believed totally in the things he believed in," Moore recalled about his father, "and he left us at least with that—a legacy of values that I think are very out of date today."[4]

Moore's formal education did very little to encourage him toward a writing career, though he recalls that he exploited his proficiency in foreign languages and English composition by writing essays for his fellow students at sixpence a throw! But his recollections of his experiences at Saint Malachy's are on the whole unpleasant and even bitter, and among other things his formal schooling served to vindicate his hostility against the parochialism already inculcated by his family and his religion. His feelings about his Jesuit education are in one sense related to the ambivalence he experiences about the whole question of religious faith, a dilemma which generates a powerful theme in his fiction, culminating in the metaphysical despair of *Catholics*. Nevertheless, we are not left in much doubt about its worst features as depicted in his second novel, *The Feast of Lupercal*, and throughout his fiction in general Moore's bitter experiences with Jesuit education have their sharp fictional recreations.

Moore was born a generation or so too late to get caught up in the rabid nationalism connected with the Irish question, a theme that informs much of fiction of such writers as Joyce, O'Flaherty, and O'Connor; he grew up feeling that the idealism represented by his father's generation was both misguided and dangerous. It was the specter of universal totalitarianisms emerging in Italy, Germany, and Russia, and given dramatic rehearsal in the Spanish Civil War, that shaped Moore's responses to the world and made him realize that the world was much larger than Ireland. "I thought my father was wrong, very much as Gavin [in *The Emperor of Ice-Cream*] thought his father was wrong," Moore recalled in an interview. "Not that I pretend to have had any foresight about Hitler, but I realized that Franco and Mussolini were not the great Christian gentlemen we were told they were."[5] During his teens he was attracted to young left-wing poets like W. H. Auden, Stephen Spender, and Louis MacNeice, who helped him see the coming holocaust and whose vision of the world very clearly helped him make his break with the Old World. Yet it should be remembered that he also liked T. S. Eliot, W. B. Yeats, and Wallace Stevens— hardly left-wing poets—so it is clear that it was their imagination and iconoclasm more than their politics that moved him. "Politically, I'm neither right, left, [nor] centre," Moore confessed in an early letter to his English publisher. "I've been all of them at times and have found flaws in all three. . . ."[6]

For the first twenty years of his life, then, Moore subconsciously stored up memories, formed opinions, and accumulated experiences which were to serve him well a decade or two later, when he was in the midst of his serious fiction. In a very real sense, the German blitzes he experienced in Belfast can be seen as both fact and symbol of his break from the stifling, parochial world represented by his family, his church, and his state. But his fiction reveals that this release, while it may have been an exciting one for the twenty-one-year-old participant at the moment it happened, in fact constitutes for Moore the novelist the occasion for searching reappraisals of its ramifications, in terms of his protagonist's relationship both to himself and to all who had a part in shaping him. *Emperor* reflects the immediate triumph of the youthful rebel, but *Limbo* and *Fergus* depict his older counterparts testing the nature of their victories, and finding themselves not all that comfortable with their conclusions.

As indicated above, the question of religious belief is very much tied in with other aspects of Moore's own life and that of his fictional protagonists. The shifts in faith in his family's life, from the Protestantism of his grandfather to the Catholicism of his father, to his own lapsed or agnostic state, undoubtedly help to account for the recurrence of this theme, and in an increasingly secular world the juxtaposition of conflicting values and beliefs has long occupied Moore's attention. Virtually all of his novels reflect this issue, even such secular ones as *Mary Dunne* and *The Doctor's Wife,* and in many respects the protagonists who are most sympathetically drawn are the ones for whom the question of belief is most central—Judith Hearne, Eileen Tierney of *Limbo,* Fergus, and Father Abbot of

Catholics. It is not that Moore has any sympathy for institutionalized religion, certainly not as it was manifested in Belfast—he has stated that "both Protestantism and Catholicism in Northern Ireland at the moment are the most desperate tragedies that can happen to people"[7] —but he has always been interested in the way that faith or belief or commitment of any sort affects the lives of ordinary people. In writing to his publisher about *Judith Hearne*, he explained that he "tried to show in a dramatic form the dilemma of faith which confronts most non-intellectual Catholics at some time or other in their lives. . . . The problems and questions raised . . . are ones which will strike an emotional response in Catholic and ex-Catholic readers."[8]

The final influence on Moore's serious fiction worth noting here is the phenomenon of exile, both as he intellectually incorporated it into his vision from writers like James Joyce, and experientially as he himself has lived his own life. As in Joyce, the exile figure in Moore is frequently both winner and loser, and in his dramatization of this dilemma, Moore reveals his understanding of its complex ramifications, and a strong sympathy for the individual who has opted for exile. Moore himself has been more or less a permanent exile since his early twenties, an option he chose quite consciously and deliberately, and this fact undoubtedly has enabled him to accept intellectually the conclusion that no one can really go home again. "Once you have exiled *yourself*," he has confessed, "it is not so easy to revoke the ukase,"[9] and on another occasion he said he saw himself as "an exile, rather than an expatriate. The exile is never going home. One place I would never live is Ireland."[10]

Moore's fiction amply documents how this dilemma is faced by a whole range of exiles—Uncle T, James Madden of *Judith Hearne*, Ginger Coffey, Brendan Tierney of *Limbo*, Fergus, and Sheila Redden of *The Doctor's Wife*, all of whom respond to their situation in vastly different ways. As with the question of faith, the assumption of exile offers no consistent or facile solution for the Moore protagonists, and characteristically there is no clear-cut triumph for these individuals. "No other postmark can compete in authority with the place of one's birth," states the nameless narrator in a Moore sketch. "It is what we fled: it may, at any time, reach up to reclaim us."[11] It is not a distortion to suggest that dilemmas like this constitute a central conflict in Moore's fiction: a kind of tug-of-war, a battle for his protagonists' souls and bodies, as it were, waged by adversaries of faith and received values on the one hand, and on the other, proponents of exile and of experiential solutions to life's problems.

III   *General Characteristics of His Fiction*

Because Moore throughout his career has been an exile from the three nations he writes about, it is not surprising that in his fiction he has developed a highly individual style and vision of experience. Indeed, not only does he not imitate other writers of Ireland, Canada, and the United States, but he does not even imitate himself from book to book. "I feel very strongly," he declared in a letter to his publisher at the very outset of his career, "that if you write you should progress in each book, not repeating yourself but tackling new problems each time."[12] To this credo he has remained faithful, for while many of his novels bear family resemblances to one another in terms of subject matter, each one creates a separate fictional world that is quite independent of the others.

Within these complex fictional worlds, inhabited by a wide range of characters, one common denominator, however, does characteristically emerge, and that is Moore's concern for the individual who exists at the edges of emptiness, uncertainty, or desperation. Judith Hearne, Mary Dunne, and Sheila Redden are poles apart in terms of individual emancipation, social status, and sexual fulfillment, but all three experience tangible fears over the question of their significance and identity; the youthful, fumbling Gavin Burke is at the opposite end of the spectrum from the venerable Abbot of Muck in respect of age and accumulated values or philosophies of life, but when the crises come upon them, they both stand staring upon the possibilities of nothingness. Diarmuid Devine, Brendan Tierney, Anthony Maloney, and Jamie Mangan are all confronted by complex and unpredictable situations to which they have to respond, and all make their response through a sense of desperation rather than through any clear understanding of ensuing consequences.

In general, the trend in Moore's fiction has been from despair to affirmation, with his protagonists moving socially from a position of entrapment toward one of emancipation, but Moore's main concern has characteristically been with the accompanying psychological dilemmas rather than with social analysis. In this respect it is interesting to note that the characters who make the least progress psychologically, Judith Hearne and Diarmuid Devine, and those who make the most, Gavin Burke and Sheila Redden, do so within the confines of, or against the backdrop of, the most oppressive of Moore's social settings, the city of Belfast. On balance, his characters have experienced failure more than triumph in their societies, and it is perhaps his exploitation of the components of failure that has earned for Moore a unique place in the world of contemporary fiction. "I think that failure is a more interesting condition than success," he stated in an early interview. "Success changes people; it makes them something they were not and dehumanizes them in a way, whereas failure leaves you with a more intense distillation of that self you are."[13]

In his later novels, the question of failure versus success is not as clear cut as it was in *Judith Hearne* and *Lupercal,* and one might be hard pressed to judge such characters as Fergus Fadden, the Abbot of Muck, or Anthony Maloney in these terms; one loses his past, one his faith, and one his life, but all three in a very real way prevail over the forces that would destroy them. The important thing is that Moore does not distort his characters by reduction, enlargement, or stereotyping, and we are thus invited to judge the dilemmas of his protagonists with a clear understanding of their talents and abilities. In the strongest meaning of these words, Moore's fiction is simple and uncomplicated: he makes his novels accessible to all readers, as Christopher Ricks cogently pointed out many years ago, "by concentrating simply, directly, and bravely on the primary sufferings and passions that everyone feels."[14]

IV *Early Writing*

During the decade between his departure from Belfast and the beginning of his writing career in Canada, Moore traveled or lived in some seventeen different nations, and, among other activities, launched out on a career in journalism, publishing his first newspaper stories in 1946. He was always attracted to fiction writing, however, and in 1949 he began his first serious story, "A Friend of the Family," out of which *Judith Hearne* eventually evolved. Though this story was never published, a *New Yorker* editor encouraged him on the strength of it to pursue his talent, and in 1951 his short story "Sassenach" was published in John Sutherland's *Northern Review.*

At that time, in order to bring in extra income, he turned his hand to pulp fiction, and in this undertaking he exploited the many experiences he had accumulated during the war and postwar periods. He had never felt a sufficiently deep involvement with the settings and actions of those events to incorporate them into his serious fiction, but their real or imagined exoticism provided the proper stuff for melodrama, and during the early part of the 1950s he produced pulp stories and novels at a steady pace, out of which he earned enough to buy time for his serious fiction. Most of the stories were published in the Montreal *Weekend Magazine* between 1951 and 1954, with others appearing in *American Magazine*, *Lilliput*, and *Bluebook*, and one of them, "The Incredible Carollers" (1952), was subsequently revised and published in the *Spectator* in 1961 as "Hearts and Flowers."

Not surprisingly, Moore wanted very much to keep his escape fiction and his serious fiction separate, and that is one reason he adopted pseudonyms for some of the seven potboiler novels he published during this period. *The Executioners* (1951) and *Wreath for a Redhead* (1951) he published under his own name, but he assumed the name Bernard Mara for *French for Murder* (1954), *A Bullet for My Lady* (1955), and *This Gun for Gloria* (1956), and Michael Bryan for *Intent to Kill* (1956) and *Murder in Majorca* (1957). It would be foolish to claim anything for most of these novels except a competent handling of the requirements of formula fiction, but *Intent to Kill* has a little more going for it than that. Set in a Montreal neurological center, it reflects an authority that probably derives from the medical backgrounds of Moore's father and brothers, which in turn provides an authenticity to the drama of the attempted murder of a populist South American president undergoing brain surgery. All this rings true, as do some of the familiar Moore landmarks: the marital discord between a conscientious surgeon and his scheming, ambitious wife, the conflict of Montreal and American values, and the capturing of the essence of a wintry Montreal in a few deft strokes, a talent Moore was later to exploit more thoroughly in his *Ginger Coffey* and *Mangan Inheritance*.

Though Moore found that the requirements of formula fiction, like his later film writing, detracted from his independence as an individual artist, it is instructive to read it, if only to appreciate how distinctly separate he was able to keep his two fictional talents. A reading of Moore's "Work and Publishing Diaries" for this phase of his career, too, reveals that he applied the same standards of personal integrity and commitment to the demands of his pulp fiction assignments as he did to his serious work: deadlines were assiduously met, revisions promptly attended to, all mechanical requirements of this lesser craft fulfilled with honesty and dispatch. This whole episode in his writing career, however, he has always viewed quite simply as a necessary drudgery, and happily, he was able simultaneously to proceed with the writing of his serious fiction and nonfiction.

CHAPTER 2

Short Stories and Nonfiction

I Short Stories

ON many occasions, Moore has acknowledged his debt to James Joyce, and perhaps nowhere is this influence more evident than in his short stories. Moore is not a prolific short-story writer—a dozen or so come to mind if we count separately published excerpts from his novels—but a half-dozen or so that he wrote during the 1950s and early 1960s rank with the best of his fiction. As in his novels, the settings of his stories shift from Belfast to Dublin, Montreal, and New York, with one uncharacteristically set in Haiti, and they deal with what we have come to expect of Moore: the grotesque, the lonely, the failure, the exile, and the tensions generated by various family relationships.

Whatever his theme, Moore utilizes for the most part a straightforward, realistic style and precisely ordered dramatic situations which lead the reader quickly into a recognition of the protagonists' particular situations. Except in his first published story, "Sassenach" (*Northern Review*, 1951), and a later fragmented confession, "Preliminary Pages for a Work of Revenge" (*Midstream*, 1961), he employs the third-person point of view throughout his short stories (indeed, as he does in all but two of his novels). He ostensibly achieves a strict objectivity through this device, but in actuality, as is the case with Joyce in *Dubliners*, it is not difficult to detect Moore's moral and ethical stances in these stories.

In "Sassenach" this stance is implicitly reflected through the sympathetic participant/narrator, who serves also as a kind of commentator at large on the moral climate of Belfast. The determinism characteristic of Moore's early novels is reflected in the components of the story's dramatic situation: the grotesque British exserviceman attempting to eke out a living on "a harsh, Ulster Sunday" by staging Houdini-like escapes on the street corner for the pennies donated by the reluctant passersby. The indifference or

24

even hostility of the Belfastians finds a kind of cosmic counterpart in the elements themselves, for just as he completes his act and begins to take up a collection, the ever-threatening downpour materializes. The crowd scurries for cover and the Sassenach—as a Protestant Englishman is disparagingly called by some Irish—is left with only a few coins for his efforts, a generous shilling of which was given by the sensitive narrator. The story anticipates *Judith Hearne* in its depiction of Belfast's lack of charity and its unremitting harshness: we sense that the citizens *might* have grudgingly given to the collection had the rain not come, but we sense, too, that the "persistent Irish rain" was on this occasion not unwelcome.

Moore's other major story with an Irish setting, "Grieve for the Dear Departed" (*Atlantic*, August 1959), on its immediate narrative level depicts a household in Dublin grieving for the dead Daniel Kelleher. But the story is really about the pride, hate, and fear generated within a family whose members are unable to communicate in any positive way with each other. The story is narrated from the point of view of the bereaved wife and mother, but in a sense the central figure is one who is never physically present in the story: the eldest son, Michael, who had left home sixteen years earlier after an irreconciled altercation with his father, and who had on the surface been the object of his unremitting hate during all those years. But, as Mrs. Kelleher came to understand, "Dan's hate was mixed with pride," and on this basis, she faked a telegram from Dan which would ensure Michael's return from America. Thus her agony stems not only from the loss of her husband, but from the guilt of her betrayal, and from what she regards in retrospect as her selfishness:

> . . . I wrote out that cable never thinking, thinking only of me, of Michael, a child I wanted to see again, cold to my husband, cold to his paralyzed face, writing down what he could no longer stop me writing, taking from him the only thing he had left, his pride, his right to hate.

This story reflects the ambivalence that runs through almost all of Moore's fiction, the tension and guilt experienced by those exiled figures who have left their home and their nation, in effect abandoning the moral values which had shaped their early lives. From a rational point of view, Michael had been justified in leaving home the way he did and in his many attempts to reconcile himself with his father over the years, and Mrs. Kelleher acted quite appropriately in luring him home. Her grief was not only for Daniel, but also for her son, the other "dear departed" of the title; yet the hold that Daniel had on them all carried over into his death, and an entire household continues to be held in bondage. In such novels as *The Emperor of Ice-Cream, An Answer from Limbo,* and *The Doctor's Wife,* Moore exploits this kind of bondage and guilt to suggest that not only a household, but an entire nation can turn this poison in on itself.

Two brief selections constitute variations on many of Moore's recurring themes, though they are not really short stories in the traditional sense, but rather confessions of sorts, of an intensely personal nature. "A Vocation" (*Tamarack Review,* Autumn 1956) formally constitutes a variation on the catechism and its implications, as played out in the consciousness of two young boys taking part in a spiritual retreat. And there is only one vocation allowable, dictated by the nature of the questions and answers, and that, as Joe concludes, is "to be a priest. An order priest, like the Dominicans or the Benedictines. It would be the safest." The comfort that this inevitable conclusion might offer is, however, offset for the reader by Moore's ironic modulation of the *in Principio* theme: "In the Beginning was the Word. And the Word was 'No.' All things came from that beginning." The story then proceeds structurally to build on what is included in "all things": God, This World, the Next World, limbo, Sin, impurity, Immortal Soul, Eternity, and Holy Communion. The spectacle of the two young boys pitting their inchoate resolutions against these awesome imponderables constitutes a poignant example of a recurring theme in Moore's fiction, the nature and role of faith, and the ambivalence toward this question that is reflected by virtually all of his protagonists.

A more bitter note is sounded in "Preliminary Pages for a Work of Revenge" (*Midstream,* Winter 1961), which in many ways can stand as an overture to a half-dozen of Moore's novels, but particularly *An Answer from Limbo, I Am Mary Dunne,* and *Fergus.* The outspoken nature of this fragmented confession, which has much in common with Dostoevsky's "Notes from Underground," is foreshadowed by its terse epigraph: "*The characters in this work are meant to be real. References to persons living and dead are intended,*" and throughout the selection the nameless first-person narrator, who seems at times to be both author and protagonist, is merciless in castigating all who have had a role in shaping him. But though, as he acknowledges, "the author does not wish to express his gratitude to anyone," he nevertheless establishes a kind of artistic credo upon the ruins of his acquaintances: "The uses he intends to make of the facts, lies, rumors, scandals and secrets so provided shall be his own. He will attempt to make his own truth for, like Pilate, he knows only that truth is not the accurate rendition of facts." Here in essence is an explanation of the relationship between autobiography or biography and fiction, and insistent throughout is the reminder that the writer is as guilty of misrepresentation as is his audience. And he does not spare his fellow writers, either, whom he calls "the small uncertain talents of our time, ever ready to arrange a panel, lunch a critic, flatter a would-be disciple. . . ."

Moore wrote this confession at that stage of his career where in effect he was making the transition from his Irish novels to those concerned primarily with North American values. The struggles he was experiencing with one of his most ambitious novels, *An Answer from Limbo,* are adumbrated here, as are what for Moore were the disturbing characteristics of the whole New York literary scene, including both the parasitic writer and his sychophantic audience. "Preliminary Pages" constitutes an important statement about the artistic process, but its intensely personal nature transforms it as well into a disturbing piece of fiction.

Moore's remaining stories all have North American settings and, for the most part, North American characters, and generally they reflect a ray of hope, or of possibility, that was by and large missing in his Irish stories. His concern is still with the individual who is somehow outside the comfortable society, whether through some physical eccentricity ("Lion of the Afternoon"), a personal affliction ("Next Thing was Kansas City"), the burden of exile ("Uncle T"), or simply a confusion stemming from the sudden conjunction of two worlds of experience ("Off the Track" and "The Sight"). In all these stories, Moore's concerns are psychological rather than sociological, though in most cases the essential nature of the society in question is invariably revealed to us.

"Lion of the Afternoon" (*Atlantic,* November 1957) was Moore's first serious story that was concerned exclusively with North American components, and, somewhat like "Sassenach," it juxtaposes the reality of grotesques against what we have come to think of as the normal world. Here an achondroplastic dwarf and his six-foot-six partner, billed predictably as "The Long And The Short Of It," transform make-believe into reality for an audience of crippled children, and triumphantly carry the day. Physically, these two are the only "abnormal" members of the performing group, and they are the only ones we see on the stage; the remainder we meet only backstage, so the audience in effect gets no chance to judge them. Ironically, the most "normal" of the entertainers, members of a Kiwanis barbershop quartet, and the only "nonprofessionals" of the group, are so conventional and stereotyped in their dress, behavior, and opinion that their "normality" is the handicap in this world. When Tait did a forward flip in front of them, they felt threatened: "Being a dwarf was enough, they felt. What they had seen, the fact that he did somersaults, somehow lowered their stature."

When Tait completes his performance, reality in a sense is momentarily transformed into make-believe, as an official, believing him to be one of the crippled children from the audience, ushers him into a playroom and gives him his gift box of toys. His response is significant: in giving the toys to the crippled boy, and then throwing the ball high into the darkness above the lighted street, he discards his dependence on everything except himself. Evident in his triumphant reentry into the real world at the end is a confidence which suggests that his "lion of the afternoon" qualities will enable him to handle whatever realities he encounters.

"Next Thing Was Kansas City" (*Atlantic*, February 1959) draws heavily on Moore's newspaper days in Montreal and anticipates *The Luck of Ginger Coffey* in the tensions it exploits between the managing editor and his assorted deskmen. The central conflict, however, revolves around what is essentially a double betrayal, a betrayal involving youth and age, innocence and experience, thoughts and deeds. There is no simple cause and effect here, however: Joe Cullen was a frequently fired lush long before he met the youthful new rewrite man, Leo, but the latter's enthusiastic boasting about his New York escapade encouraged Joe to believe he had found a soulmate to join him in his rebellion against the managing editor. When Leo betrays him not only by refusing to acknowledge his responsibility for Joe's drunken state (not unlike Devine's betrayal of Una in *The Feast of Lupercal*) but also by refusing to join him against McAlmon, Cullen commits his act of betrayal: he came over, confronted Leo, and "smiled into terrified baby-blue eyes. The Judas smile of love."

In his description of Joe's alcoholism, Moore compels us to recognize the pathos of his situation, and just how precarious the balance is that he is attempting to maintain:

Rivers of broken blue veins mapped on the thick red skin of nose and cheeks. Joe's facial tic, irregular, jumping now with the excitement of drinks and boasts. And the things to hide it: the well-brushed white hair, the neat blue suit, the clean shirt and black tie. Careful neatness, mocked by those minute abrasions, by that tiny jumping fold of flesh in Joe's cheek.

Just as Joe attempted to disguise his problem by an outward show of "careful neatness," Leo attempted to overcome his problem of youthful inexperience by an outward show of bravado. Throughout the story, his "baby-blue eyes" are emphasized: he is essentially childlike in his failure to understand the moral implications of what he is doing. His innocence both clashes and joins forces with Cullen's experience, but neither can cope with the reality of McAlmon's ultimatum. In a sense, Joe's penalty will be easier to bear than Leo's for he, after all, has been fired many times before. Leo, on the other hand, has just surrendered his innocence, and "his terrified baby-blue eyes" at the end suggest the nature of the guilt he is doomed to carry with him and attempt to resolve.

This theme of unwitting betrayal constitutes the major conflict in "Off the Track," a story Moore wrote for the 1960 CBC "Wednesday Night" series, and published the following year. On the surface it is merely a depiction of a touristy Canadian sociologist and his wife attempting to film natives and their way of life off the beaten tourist path in Haiti, for which they had prepared themselves by taking summer courses at the University of Toronto. The last thing that Alex and Margaret Cole wanted was to be mistaken for tourists, especially American tourists, but Moore's initial description of them shows the futility of this hope:

Alex Cole carried a Rolleiflex around his neck and a light meter stuck like a watch fob out of the pocket of his white shirt. Margaret wore a bright straw hat purchased in a tourist shop in Port-au-Prince.

But the story quickly takes on a threatening aspect, for as the Coles move further toward an isolated village, layers of fear, uncertainty, and incomprehensibility begin to surround them, though they are not always astute enough to read these signs for what they mean. Thus, in the story's central episode, though they know about the Haitian's distrust and fear of a camera, they nevertheless film a whole series of shots of a young boy, and bribe him with a silver coin to boot. The boy's punishment is as swift and horrible as it is inevitable: the violent thrashing he receives and his surrendering of the coin evoke the scene of punishment for betrayal in Prosper Merimée's "Mateo Falcone," though Moore's story lacks the unspeakable horror of that Corsican tale.

At the end, Alex Cole has a sufficient sensitivity toward this world they had invaded to leave his film behind, and he hangs his empty camera around his neck in an act of penance, as it were. Margaret, however, really fails to understand what has happened, or why it happened, and she moves quickly from hysteria to the comfort of a cliché: "Well," she said. "we've found out one thing. They're certainly a horse of a different colour down here, aren't they?"

Moore is not as familiar with the social fabric of Haiti as he is with that of Belfast, Montreal, or New York, and perhaps for that reason this story has more artifice than art about it, and it lacks the sense of involvement and sympathy which characterizes his other stories, particularly, as we will see, his longest one, "Uncle T." But "Off the Track" transcends the limitations of mere formula fiction in the degree to which Moore develops the human qualities of the Coles: he has clearly observed many tourists, and he has here looked beneath their superficial appearance and discovered elements of sensitivity, but also of ordinariness and obtuseness.

Moore gets back into more familiar territory in his finely wrought "Uncle T" (*Gentleman's Quarterly*, November 1960), the longest and undoubtedly the best story he has written, and one that, like "Grieve for the Dear Departed," has its genesis in the hate and pride existing within the confines of a family. Ireland, Canada, and New York are all involved here, with the essential conflicts surfacing in and between families of two generations—Vincent Bishop and his Canadian bride, Barbara, and Uncle T (Turlough Carnahan) and his American wife, Bernadette. But behind both husbands lie irreconciled conflicts with their Irish fathers, for both Vincent and Uncle T share a rebellious nature and an anticlericalism that led to their exile from home and country. Much of the poignancy of this story resides in the discrepancy between Vincent's idealistic impressions of Uncle T, accumulated over three years through their exchange of letters, and the actuality of their confrontation in New York. Barbara and Bernadette are involved witnesses to this confrontation, and their separate comments to their husbands as the evening drags on undoubtedly reflect the unpleasant truths about the Carnahans; their comments also, however, foreshadow the irreconcilable conflict that lies ahead, the foundations of which have already taken shape in the brief married life of Vincent and Barbara.

Yet as in "Grieve for the Dear Departed" and in such novels as *The Emperor of Ice-Cream* and *Fergus,* questions keep coming back to haunt us about the real nature of family relationships, even though rationally we know that Barbara and Bernadette are right. They are of course not without fault—charity, as Uncle T reminds them, is seriously lacking in both, and Barbara, a two-day bride, evinces no sympathy for Vincent's dilemma. Ironically, Vincent's generous surrender to his uncle at the end of the story—an act brought about by his bitter recollection of how his own father had rejected him—may jeopardize his own marriage beyond repair, but it will momentarily sustain Uncle T's illusion about himself, a truth which for Vincent at this moment assumes an overriding priority.

The relationship between Vincent and his uncle evokes the doppelgänger motif and the curse of inherited legacies that Moore was to develop more fully later on in *The Mangan Inheritance.* "I have long thought that you," Uncle T had written in a letter to Vincent, "—a rebel, a wanderer and a lover of literature—must be very much like me when I was your age," and at their first meeting he insists upon the resemblance between them. Initially, Vincent is somewhat outraged at this suggestion, but as the evening wears on they find themselves increasingly in league with each other. The spectacle that greets him as he turns from the taxi is a disturbing one:

There, half-drunk on the pavement, stood a fat old man with dyed hair. Where was the boy who once wrote poems, the young iconoclast who once spoke out against the priests? What had done this to him? Was it drink, or exile, or this marriage to a woman twenty years his junior? Or had that boy never been?

These questions, quite clearly, might as easily be addressed to himself, and it is this realization that constitutes the terror of his situation. Like so many of the protagonists in Moore's North American fiction, Vincent will have to resolve the conflicts between the realities of his present world and the legacies from a distant time and place that have come down to him with a distorted shape and the crippling nature of a family curse. That "Uncle T" does not show Vincent resolving this issue is of course both a source of its power and a reflection of the psychological realities of the state of exile that Moore probably understands as well as any writer today.

That Moore waited over a decade and a half before producing his next short story gives some support to his frequently expressed view

that he is not really at ease with this genre, though, as with his
earlier stories, his craft here belies his protestation. For "The Sight,"
specially written for a 1977 collection entitled *Irish Ghost Stories*,[1] is
a cleverly wrought tale in which the supernatural, as in novels like
Fergus and *The Mangan Inheritance*, intensifies but does not
replace the underlying realism. It is unlike most of his other short
stories in that the immediate social world of the protagonist and his
own past actions do not, as they do for example in "Uncle T,"
logically help to explain the crisis that comes suddenly upon him—
unless, of course, we interpret the story as a moral fable wherein
past sins bring about their inevitable punishments.

On the surface, Benedict Chipman's medical situation is a fairly
routine matter, and all the rational evidence that he can muster
should support him in this diagnosis. But this logic is suddenly
undercut by the irrational prognostications of his clairvoyant house-
keeper, Mrs. Leahy, whose power of "sight" enabled her to dream
of his death, a gift she had successfully demonstrated numerous
times in the past. This supernatural intrusion constitutes a sudden
and unmanageable element for Chipman, a confident and wealthy
lawyer who up to this point in his life had taken from the world,
without conscience, whatever he desired. He had on one occasion
seduced his brother's wife; his frequent womanizing had directly
contributed to his own wife's death in an alcoholic clinic, and he
himself realizes "that his interest in other people was limited to the
extent of their contributions to his purse, his pleasure or his self-
esteem."

Thus this man, who had used everybody as he wished, and who
stood in arrogant independence from family, colleagues, and former
friends, suddenly becomes totally dependent on Mrs. Leahy, whom
he regards as an "ignorant, stupid old creature with her hedgehog
eyes and butterfat brogue . . . [and] primitive folk nonsense, typi-
cally Irish. . . ." Yet she has in a sense the power of life and death
over him, and his realization that he cannot ever escape from this
hold both terrifies and transforms him into a creature who can
suddenly be moved by love and gentleness. "Tears, the unfamiliar
tears of dependence, blurred his vision: made the room tremble.
Gently, she nodded her head." Ironically, therefore, the "sight"
which she possesses has in a sense been transferred to him, and its
accompanying transmogrification enables him even in his blurred
vision to recognize the reality of his own mortality.

In spite of Moore's reservations, the half-dozen or so stories discussed here do not bespeak any incompetence with this genre, and we recall, too, that his powerful *Catholics* was originally published as a sixty-page novella in the *New American Review*. Clearly, when Moore chooses the shorter fictional form, he knows its requirements and its conventions, and he shapes his art accordingly. "When Brian Moore is at his best," the editor of the *Atlantic* said in 1956, "there is nobody of his age that is better."[2] He was speaking specifically of "Lion of the Afternoon," but this assessment is equally applicable to many of his other short stories as well.

II *Nonfiction*

Moore has produced a surprisingly large body of nonfiction, in the form of literary criticism, journalism, essays, travel pieces, and occasional pieces, as well as two books, *Canada* and *The Revolution Script*. His shorter pieces have appeared in a wide range of publications, from daily newspapers to magazines like the *Atlantic*, *Holiday*, and *Nova*, but to date he has resisted the tendency shown by many writers to collect these miscellaneous writings in book form. This is a pity, for many are hidden away in obscure or out-of-print journals, and the best of his nonfiction reveals a witty, urbane, and incisive writer whose thorough research and willingness to address himself to controversial issues give these pieces more than a local or passing importance.

A. *Journalist Writings*

The earliest record of Moore's writings takes the form of two newspaper stories written in Warsaw in November 1946, and published in the *Dublin Sunday Independent*. Written while he was with the UNRRA Mission in Poland, these stories were secretly sent out of Warsaw via British Diplomatic Bag service, for they described events which were threats to the Soviet-backed regime in Poland. One dealt with the disappearance from Poland of the leader of the Polish Peasant party, the major democratic political opposition at the time, and the other with the conflict between the Communist government and the Roman Catholic Church in Poland. There is nothing significant about these two pieces of journalism in any literary sense, but in terms of Moore's career they constitute the beginning of a journalistic interest which has surfaced at regular intervals throughout his life and has characteristically manifested itself in a sympathetic understanding of the problem of political and social injustice, whether in Ireland, Canada, or the United States.

This trait was to be most fully exemplified in *The Revolution Script*, discussed below, but it revealed itself as well in many of Moore's occasional pieces, and in his reviews of books concerned with such revolutionary groups as the Black Panthers and the FLQ.

There is a clear link here between Moore's nonfiction and his fiction in his championing, if not of the victim of a deliberately vindictive and repressive society, then certainly of the underdog, of the person who on many counts is one of life's losers. Moore's devastating essay on the problems in Ulster[3] was published over a dozen years after he created Judith Hearne and Diarmuid Devine, but reading it as sociology leads us inevitably back to those early fictional protagonists and enables us to understand more clearly the social forces that shaped them. Similarly, his retrospective recollection of Montreal after a decade's residence there[4] captures aspects of that city's atmosphere and social realities that undoubtedly influenced his fictional creation of Ginger Coffey, with which he was simultaneously engaged. In these and other occasional pieces, Moore's treatment of his subject matter reflects both a thorough research and a compassionate attitude, though with some of his more trivial topics, like the Dublin horse show[5] or California's expensive reducing salons,[6] he indulges in a genial humor or a whimsical satire.

His best journalism, like his best fiction, reflects his strong personal involvement with the particular situation and its participants, and this approach is evident even in what must have been his most diffuse journalistic assignment, his book on Canada, written in conjunction with the Editors of *Life*.[7] It constitutes on the whole a sensitive and detached overview of Canada's development as a nation, and it gives assessments of Canadians and Canadian institutions that perhaps an indigenous writer would miss. Moore, I think, is wrong on some crucial points, such as his claim that French-Canada has not produced any truly indigenous art: his selection of Hémon's *Maria Chapdelaine* rather than, say, Ringuet's *Trente Arpents*, as representative of French-Canadian fiction, and his singling out of Longfellow's "Evangeline" rather than the powerful poetry of Hector de Saint-Denys-Garneau or Anne Hébert suggests he was perhaps depending unduly on popular opinion about Québecois literature. There is always a risk, of course, in writing a book according to the editorial party line of an influential American magazine, and occasionally we seem to be reading what the editors of *Life* want its American readers to read. But for the most part

Moore's observations on Canada are refreshing in their sense of discovery and blunt in suggesting some of the problems faced both by Canadians and by those who try to understand them:

[Canadians] have been lectured, advised, warned and dismissed by a stream of professors, novelists, poets and pundits, many of them Americans or Britons, whose ignorance of Canada's problems has been matched only by their sublime condescension. (131)

It is for the historian to pass judgment on *Canada*'s value as history; for the general reader, because Moore does not really have any axes to grind, or any *a priori* historical biases, and perhaps particularly for the new arrival in Canada, the book serves as a useful and stimulating document.

A much stronger sense of personal involvement, however, is evident in the two pieces Moore wrote about his country of birth, and one can readily detect an intensification of his feelings between his 1964 essay on Belfast[8] and the 1970 essay on Ulster. The earlier one was more than a tourist piece, though its publication in *Holiday* probably required a somewhat uncritical approach, but we sense Moore's discomfort behind some of his cheerful prose, and his conclusion that, in spite of bitter religious and social conflict, the people of Belfast will endure—"they can stick it. Aye." His later essay blends personal reminiscence and blunt documentary reportage and provides a disturbing diagnosis indeed of the plight of Ulster. He concedes that his erstwhile countrymen may question his credentials to talk about the situation:

And who am I to talk? A Catholic who is no longer a Catholic, an Ulsterman who holds a Canadian passport and lives in California, an Irishman who has lived longer out of Ireland than he has lived in it. What can I know of Ulster's present troubles?

One answer is that he knows that Ulster's present troubles are not much different from Ulster's past troubles, which he himself lived through as a youth: "Riots. The same old riots we had in my childhood. Mobs of rampaging Protestant *lumpenproletariat* trying to terrorize their equally ignorant Catholic *lumpenproletariat* neighbors. . . . Ordinary people set against ordinary people because there is something old and rotten still alive here." But another answer to his question is that he knows about it because of the medium of television: he sees the same British soldiers here that he saw six thousand miles away in his California living room, and in effect, millions of people all over the world become instant experts on Ulster's troubles. Television, what Moore calls "the agitprop of modern revolt," not only communicates what is going on, but it creates its own version of this reality, and of course, since "the whole world is watching," it inspires fanatics of all sorts to have their go at revolution. Moore is far from being a McLuhanite, but his belief in the role of television in shaping a crisis is increasingly evident in his works—most notably in *The Revolution Script* but also in novels like *Catholics* and *The Great Victorian Collection*.

The dilemma in a situation such as he describes in "Bloody Ulster" is that television must continue to nourish what it "begat," and Moore, driving through Belfast and nearing his former home, articulates his realization of this point: "I remember the first evening I saw this fuss on television. There, far away in California, I sensed an exile's truth, that truth which now homes in on me. This news item is dying: if it dies, nothing will change here." His solution—that "it must escalate [and] blood must run in the streets"—on one level is a hyperbolic response to the bankruptcy of the present Ulster regime, but on another level it reflects the logic of a world that is increasingly governed by a television-created reality.

B. *Literary Criticism*

In a review of Mary McCarthy's *On the Contrary*,[9] Moore concedes the link between fiction and journalism that he himself was to pursue in *The Revolution Script*, reminding us that the novel had its origins in the reportage of things that were true. He praises her essay "The Fact in Fiction," but does not wholly subscribe to its premises, enjoining us to remember that it was not merely "chunks of fact which gave the nineteenth-century novels their wondrous solidity." A reminder, perhaps, that we should not try too hard to make his own "piece of reportage" a work of fiction.

Characteristically, most of Moore's book reviews—and out of the twenty or so he wrote, about twelve gave him the occasion for literary speculation—can also be read as implicit comments on his own fiction, which is probably what happens when a novelist turns critic. It is unfortunate, I think, that of all the forms of writing he has indulged in throughout his career, it is only here that he has not written at any extended length, for his reviews provide consistent evidence of a widely read person, and of a perceptive and far-ranging intelligence.

Fairly evenly divided among Canadian, American, and British/Irish books, Moore's reviews complement his own peregrinations, and not infrequently he explores writers who, like himself, have experienced situations of exile. He is harsher on British writers than he is on Americans and Canadians: John Fowles's *The Magus* and Anthony Powell's *Valley of Bones* get particularly short shrift, while Malcolm Lowry's *Hear Us O Lord* and Robertson Davies's *The Manticore* receive high praise.

Many years ago, Moore made a comment which seems particularly pertinent to the reviews: "A good writer must feel sympathetic with even the least of his characters, and it is only the second-rate writer who will make out of his flat characters mere caricatures."[10] It is on these grounds that he castigates Powell, and he takes the opportunity as well to attack aspects of the class system which he feels militate against the artistic development of many British novelists. Powell, he feels, commits a kind of fictional immorality by creating characters for whom he has no compassion, protagonists whose standards, according to Moore, "are, quite simply, the cruel, adolescent judgments of the English public school where style is all, . . . where, in a curious Gresham's Law of snobbery, charm drives out sincerity and the hounding of inferiors stands out as wit." This is a harsh judgment—not perhaps the equal of his unpublished review of John Braine's *Jealous God*, turned down by *Life* because it was "too harsh"—but it is consistent with the attitudes he displays toward his own unpleasant characters, such as Bernie Rice, Ernie Truelove, or Fred X. Vaterman, all of whom it must have been tempting to caricature.

Christopher Ricks has described Moore as a Victorian novelist, so it is not surprising to find him praising Robertson Davies, whom he sees as "a living, breathing Victorian," come to put our fictional house in order. "The Novel House is empty," Moore announces. "Its tenants have wandered witlessly out into Barthian byways, through Borgesian mazes, to squat, disconsolate, at Beckett's crossroads, waiting for some faceless God." I suspect this is as much a comment on the landlord as it is on the tenants, but for the time being, Davies, with his comfortable furniture of melodrama, coincidence, omniscient narrator, and so on, will provide a welcome change from the recent confusion. Sincerity and compassion are Davies's hallmarks, and if he is unable to fill the house with his own kind, "at least," Moore concludes, "he has dared to go back inside, all the way up to the room at the top of the stairs."

Moore's "Novel House," however, is not restricted to Victorians. Gabrielle Roy is admitted, with her straightforward realistic novel, *The Tin Flute,* and so is Malcolm Lowry, who, in his surrealistic *Hear Us O Lord,* has "found ways to narrate his lostness as few expatriate writers have ever done." The essayist and critic Edmund Wilson, "remembered as an eagle with a formidable cultural wingspan," is welcome, in part because of his incisive analysis of the anticlericalism in Québecois literature, yet one of the most formidable of these disciples, Marie-Claire Blais, is a bit too manipulative in her *St. Lawrence Blues* to gain admittance at this time. John Fowles would probably get in with *Daniel Martin,* but he disqualified himself with *The Magus,* which had, for Moore's taste, "too much hocus in the pocus." And a fellow exile, Clark Blaise, protests a bit too much in his *A North American Education,* and Moore suspects he would be ill at ease with this heterogenous company.

In a review of Malcolm Cowley's *Exile's Return,* Moore cautions us against an inward-turning tendency that can quickly transpose us from provincialism to parochialism. The great writers of the 1920s, he reminds us, "were not nationals of their countries but members of a brotherhood. Now that it is dead, an ugly literary nationalism replaces it." While this is true only in part—Hemingway remains American, Joyce Irish, and Callaghan Canadian, in spite of their "lost generation" affiliations—Moore's point is well taken and it helps to explain his own hesitancy to become identified with any literary movements of the three nations that have shaped him. The essays and reviews examined here, however, clearly bespeak his familiarity with the respective literary and social scenes, and even a documentary novel like *The Revolution Script* demonstrates his consistent striving for a literature that transcends the parochial.

C.   The Revolution Script *(1971)*[11]

Interestingly, just as "Bloody Ulster" was being published, another violent drama was in the making in Quebec, and within weeks Moore was in Montreal watching, along with the rest of Canada, the unfolding of a revolution on television. "What really captivates me," Moore said later, "is the fact that we've entered a curiously theatrical era in politics. Trudeau succeeded in coming to power because he's a magnificent actor on television and a handful of FLQ succeeded in making a revolution because of the existence of the media."[12]

This was one of the notions that inspired Moore to write his second nonfiction book about Canada; the other was the anonymity of the main protagonists of his drama—the six members of the Liberation cell and the four members of the Chenier cell who among them changed the moral climate of Canada overnight: suddenly kidnapping, political murder, terrorism, and police-state laws became factors in the everyday lives of Canadians.

Moore selected his working title for this book—*The Six Kids' Revolution*—from the words of the kidnapped James Cross, who said, upon his release, "It was a case of six kids trying to make a revolution."[13] The facts that Moore used as the skeleton of his book were derived from the events as they happened, and his faithful use of such documentary evidence as the FLQ communiqués, a ninety-minute tape left by the kidnappers, and various media releases gives to his book a strong reportorial authenticity. But like many others who watched the crisis unfold on television screens, Moore was strongly conscious of the anonymity or "faceless" condition of the kidnappers. He therefore set out to rewrite the script of this event, with the intention, as he stated in a prefatory note to his book, to use "the techniques of fiction to bring these young revolutionaries on stage."

In this respect, *The Revolution Script* is a convincing success, for without unduly enlarging or romanticizing them, Moore sympathetically dramatizes the conditions and frustrations that led them to this moment of their lives. Moore never met any of these FLQ members personally, and thus in a sense they remained for him fictional characters rather than real personalities, so he retained the novelist's freedom to do with them what he wanted. "They were marvellous," he confided in an interview with Donald Cameron; "they'd disappeared into history, and they weren't going to talk back. So this is sort of an ideal situation actually, and I seized it with a certain amount of ruthlessness."[14] As a result, the motives and actions of the FLQ members assume much more complexity than was suggested by the public explanations of Messrs. Bourassa, Sharp, and Trudeau. Moore dramatizes the human and domestic conflicts between Jacques Cosette-Trudel and his wife, Louise; between Louise and her brother Jacques Lanctot; the ideological growth of the cell's oldest member, Marc Carbonneau; and the struggle within the youthful Yves Langlois between his frustrated sexual desires and his restrictive revolutionary code. "The reality is hoping I'll see a girl undress," he muses at one point. "The unreality is not knowing if, in the next forty-eight hours, I will be chosen to kill that man next door, a man old enough to be my father" (51). Though he does not realize it, this issue for Yves and the other revolutionaries is philosophically related to what Camus saw as the central question in *The Rebel:* "To find out whether innocence, the moment it becomes involved in action, can avoid committing murder."[15]

The "facelessness" of these revolutionaries, Moore clearly implies, is not merely a deliberate or accidental by-product of television coverage; it is rather a manifestation of the sociological and political fact that, in spite of the Quiet Revolution and in spite of the "liberalism" of the Bourassas, the Trudeaus, and the Drapeaus, privilege and the class system are as strongly entrenched in Quebec as they were in the dark days of the Duplessis regime. Moore clearly sees a parallel between the situation in Quebec and that in Ulster, and his real concern over Trudeau's imposition of the War Measures Act has its roots in his familiarity with the Special Powers Act in Ulster, introduced in the early days of the Irish revolution and never rescinded.

The Revolution Script is not to be judged as fiction, of course; even as a documentary novel, the reader is apt to say, "Give me the documents instead." It is, quite bluntly, an exercise in propaganda, a counterstatement to the official establishment account of the events as they were unfolding, and it is on the level of this collision of interpretations that it assumes fictional qualities. Like fiction, it intrigues and unsettles us because of the different versions of truth and reality it communicates, and leaves us with the unanswerable question of whether Moore's script is any less or any more reliable than the establishment script, or indeed, whether any of the scripts capture the real truth of the events. The book does not resolve these questions but, like good fiction, it raises them and brings them to a point where political reality begins to assume a philosophical dimension.

The Revolution Script has had its problems with the critics, either because they took it as literal journalism or because they tried to wrench it into fiction. To argue, as Jeanne Flood does,[16] that it basically constitutes a continuation of the father-son conflict, with the fathers (Trudeau, Cross, Laporte) being defeated by their revolutionary "sons," is to indulge in an intriguing, but fanciful speculation, for the evidence simply does not support such a reading. The book clearly suggests, for example, that the death of Laporte can be blamed in some part on the inactivity of his fellow politicians, especially Bourassa. And Trudeau, like that other Machiavellian politician in Moore's fiction, Reverend Keogh in *The Feast of Lupercal*, not only puts down a revolution but strengthens his house in the process. As for Cross, Moore's final words are significant: "It was, perhaps, the final irony in this Canadian drama. Two men had been kidnapped. The French Canadian lay dead. The Englishman went free" (261). A critic writing in the *Partisan Review*, too, tries to invest the book with too much fictional significance, though his point that *The Revolution Script* is "the product of a continuous concern in Moore's work with *nous autres* and the potentialities of liberation"[17] has merit, particularly if we see liberation in psychological and personal rather than political terms, for then novels like *Judith Hearne, Lupercal, Ginger Coffey,* and *The Emperor of Ice-Cream* can be pressed into service. Of all his novels, it is only in *Catholics* where politics—and there it is politics of a special kind—assumes a significant role. Politics in the *Partisan Review* sense *is* central in *The Revolution Script*, in essays like "Bloody Ulster," and in reviews of books like Huey Newton's *Revolutionary Suicide* and Malcolm Reid's *The Shouting Signpainters*, and it is in this journalistic strain that the continuity resides. His modesty notwithstanding, Moore may be right in denying *The Revolution Script* an integral place in his work and in claiming it as "a piece of reportage,"[18] but it nevertheless constitutes an inevitable and powerful expression of an attitude toward a political and social reality which has shaped many of his fictional protagonists.

CHAPTER 3

Old World Perspectives

I *Introduction*

IN much the same way that Joyce succeeded in *Dubliners* in writing "a chapter of the moral history of [his] country," Brian Moore in his first two and his fifth novels added a further chapter to that history about a city that clearly supersedes Joyce's Dublin as Ireland's "centre of paralysis." *Judith Hearne* (1955), *The Feast of Lupercal* (1957), and *The Emperor of Ice-Cream* (1965) constitute as much a moral history of Belfast as they do a fictional portrait of the inhabitants of that narrow and mean city, though in the first two of these novels particularly these strains are in effect inseparable. Belfast has unmistakably imposed its destructive traits of bigotry and privation upon its Judith Hearnes, its Diarmuid Devines, and, in Gavin Burke's case, upon the individuals who attempt to confine him, but it is equally clear that in their narrow attitudes toward the world at large, in their fearful and inward-turning habits of life and thought, these individuals collectively are responsible for Belfast's being such a mean and spiritless city. More than in any of his other novels, Moore in these works effected an artistic fusion of psychological individual and sociological milieu, and, indeed, the reader is hard pressed to apply with any assurance the conventional judgments of cause and effect.

In large part, this accomplishment is closely related to the pervasive realism of these novels, particularly of *Judith Hearne* and *Lupercal*, to the faithfulness with which Moore portrays character and place, with the result that the reader is constantly reminded of the appropriateness or even the inevitability of a given event or situation. This approach not only compels the reader to believe in the reality of Belfast, but it allowed Moore to resolve his own attitude toward that city and that part of his life:

Judith Hearne was written during one Canadian summer in 1953 and to my surprise I discovered in writing it what I really felt about my past. I left

42

Ireland with the intention of not going back, but my reasons became clear
only when I wrote that first novel. It was then that my bitterness against
the Catholic Church, my bitterness against the bigotry in Northern Ireland,
my feelings about the narrowness of life there and, in a sense, my loneliness
when living as an exile in Canada all focussed to produce a novel about
what I felt the climate of Ulster to be.[1]

For Moore, these novels undoubtedly had a purgative and consoling
effect: though exile was a lonely state, it was an infinitely better
existence than that experienced by his early Belfast protagonists,
whose lives were characterized chiefly by illusion and defeat.

Judith and Devine are in a very literal sense victims of a fixed
order, and the powerful impact created by these protagonists derives
in part from their pathetic and futile attempts to make meaningful
moves in a world that resists all moves that are not prescribed. The
determinism which operates here is cosmic in its effect, as it were,
but it is social in its derivation, and is made manifest in all the
confrontations that Judith and Dev experience. There is a strange
blending of paralysis and willful self-destruction residing in their
actions, a condition that reflects the state of the city itself, so that
the characters are not merely helpless pawns in some cosmic game:
they very clearly contribute to the unfolding of their own fate. Both
Judith and Devine operate on a combination of memory, desire,
illusion, and hope, and neither one can act decisively on the moment
which could change this. At the end of the respective novels, both
are very much in the same position as they were at the beginning,
though ironically they have achieved a stronger grasp on their own
state of reality, brought about by the further erosion of their
illusions.

In terms of their talents, accomplishments, and social standing
within the Belfast community, Judith, Dev, and Gavin are poles
apart; Judith is in all respects one of life's losers, with no attributes
whatsoever to salvage her, whereas Dev and Gavin have a number
of qualities which sustain them. Nevertheless, their dilemmas are
identical in one crucial respect—all three are sexually chaste, and
thus are in a significant respect incomplete individuals. All of
Moore's novels (except *Catholics*, which clearly has other concerns)
demonstrate the importance of a healthy sexuality as a component
of human maturity and fulfillment, and it is interesting to note that
it is only in these three Belfast novels where the protagonists remain
chaste. Where all possibility of sexual initiation has passed, as in

Judith Hearne and *Lupercal,* the effect tends toward the tragic;
where it has not yet happened, but is imminent, as it were, as in
Emperor, the effect is toward the comic. The fact that these two
situations exist in novels with identical settings suggests of course
that Moore's vision is a flexible one, and that his early determinism
was more sociologically oriented than philosophical. Moore has
perhaps become a different writer in moving away from the despair
of *Judith Hearne* and *Lupercal,* but he has rarely surpassed that
early artistic achievement. His aesthetic at that time, therefore,
cannot be dismissed as an apprenticeship or inchoate stance, but
must be seen as representing a view of experience which was both
experiential and profoundly held.

In these two earlier novels, Moore reflects very much the influence of Joyce, particularly in the way he juxtaposes his characters
against the pervasive sterility of the Irish environment. The influence, in terms of both the theme and the underlying naturalism
which inform these books, is clearly that of *Dubliners,* though
Moore's world does not allow for the sense of life that Joyce's
Dublin did. There is no one in either *Judith Hearne* or *Lupercal,* for
example, who reflects the spirit, say, of the narrators of "An
Encounter" or "Araby," or of Gretta Conroy of "The Dead "; the
comparison inevitably depends on Marion of "Clay," Little Chan-
dler of "A Little Cloud," or James Duffy of "A Painful Case," all of
whom have missed out on the possibilities of life. And one has only
to compare the boarding house in Joyce's story of that name with
Mrs. Rice's in *Judith Hearne* to grasp the difference between an
alive Dublin and a sterile Belfast: in Dublin there is love, there is
bawdry, there is laughter and hope; there are only suspicion,
hostility, and ignorance in Moore's Belfast. On the whole, these
Belfast novels unrelievedly depict the paralysis of that city and
present a far grimmer chapter of Ireland's moral history than does
Joyce's *Dubliners.*

II   Judith Hearne *(1955)*[2]

General opinion still holds, a quarter of a century after its
publication, that *Judith Hearne* remains as one of Moore's most
successful novels, in terms both of its powerful delineation of
character and of its disciplined craftsmanship, and the claim has
been made that it is "perhaps the best novel to come out of
Northern Ireland."[3] It is an extremely restricted novel in terms of

the fictional canvas covered and the human actions that are involved, and no cosmic reverberations or Nietzschean figures disturb the universe that Moore creates here. Indeed, it derives its power from concentration and contraction, rather than from the diffusion and expansion which characterize such classic examples of the naturalistic novel as Zola's *L'Assommoir* or Dreiser's *An American Tragedy*. Yet in its depiction of how one of life's losers is perpetually frustrated by forces she cannot control, *Judith Hearne* reflects a determinism that is every bit as pervasive as the more cosmic variety.

Judith Hearne grew out of an unpublished short story called "A Friend of the Family," which Moore had toyed with as early as 1949, and of which he completed three separate versions between 1951 and 1953. Moore obviously felt close to his material here,[4] for the "friend" in fact was a longtime companion of his family, a Mary Judith Keogh, an eccentric spinster given to the wearing of reds and the drinking of unwatered whiskeys, who died in her eighties after carefully arranging the details of her own funeral. Moore relied extensively on his family's recollections about Miss Keogh, and it is rewarding to trace the fictional creation of Judith Hearne out of this unusual figure and to see how Moore fleshed out the framework of the original story.

In the story version, the setting is Dublin rather than Belfast, with the main action taking place between Judith and the Brannigan family; the fact that both she and Professor Brannigan are in their seventies feeds her illusion, but not his, that their original liaison was a romantic one. Judith dies from the complications brought on by bronchitis and by her regular use of whiskey, which, she assures Moira, she takes "merely to cut the phlegm." Madden appears briefly in the story, as a doorman who has never been abroad, but his main role is to procure for Judith a brand of whiskey known colloquially as "sheet lightning," for which service he is rewarded in her will. Miss Hearne's greatest moment is her funeral, for which she has made out the guest list, and unlike her counterpart in the novel, for whom the family graveyard is closed, she is buried alongside her ancestors in the most appropriate fashion.

In contrast to the unrelentingly grim *Judith Hearne*, "A Friend of the Family" stands essentially as a comic sketch, for what we are left with is Judith's graveside triumph over Moira Brannigan and over her own lifelong obeisance to propriety and respectability.

Moore's task in the novel was a far more formidable one, and in a letter to his English publisher he set forth some of the problems as he saw them:

[*Judith Hearne*] is perhaps a "joyless" difficult book, but it is one which has been in my mind for a very long time and which I feel I had to write. I chose a difficult type of heroine, I admit, but I wished to avoid the autobiographical type of first novel. . . . I tried to show in a dramatic form the dilemma of faith which confronts most non-intellectual Catholics at some time or other in their lives.

It is also a book about a woman, presenting certain problems of living peculiar to women. I write it with all the sympathy and understanding I am capable of and I think that among the people who have read it so far, no woman has disliked it. I think it is a book for women to read because they understand the viewpoint, and for my own sex, it is an effort to help men gain a greater understanding of women like Miss Hearne.

I make no apology for its being about an uninteresting woman. Miss Hearne is meant to bore and irritate the reader at times. Real people do. There is far too much of a vogue at the moment for books about one-eyed men, whores and other assorted weirdies—for phony sensationalism— which I feel has little or nothing to do with life as it is lived by most of us.[5]

Judith Hearne points forward to a number of concerns explored from different perspectives by Moore in much of his later fiction. Though the social worlds of their protagonists are vastly different from that which entraps Judith, both *I Am Mary Dunne* and *The Doctor's Wife* examine very closely the particular problems involved in being a woman in a world that is seemingly ordered for and by men. And most of Moore's novels, but particularly *Limbo, Fergus,* and *Catholics,* take up the complex question of the place of faith in the life of ordinary people. What *Judith Hearne* loses by the relative lack of complexity with which it explores these concerns, it gains from the directness of Moore's realism as it conveys the poignancy of Judith's situation. Though in the literal sense she cuts a ridiculous figure, Moore manipulates both the objective third-person point of view and the minute details of her dreary existence to elicit the reader's compassion rather than any sense of superiority.

In the tradition of the naturalist, Moore sets in motion the components of Judith's final illusions and decline by establishing a logical and convincing relationship between her actions and her environment. Judith operates essentially within the three institutions of Belfast which not only in a literal sense reflect her social, religious, and personal status and hopes, but which ironically, by novel's end, have conspired together to thrust her beyond the possibility of achieving any kind of personal fulfillment, and in the process surrendering their individual roles to an institution which can only administer impersonally to her inevitable demise. Her "furnished room" in Earnscliffe Home represents the beginning again of a cycle—and probably the final cycle—that Judith has become all too familiar with, but this time it is at a lower level not so much of reality, for her earlier rejection of her aunt and of the Church has ironically strengthened her hold on reality, but rather at a lower level of sustenance. But she cannot summarily dismiss a lifetime of habits: though she has renounced the two forces that have held her in bondage, she arranges once again her aunt's picture and the Sacred Heart in a kind of vestigial response to a lifetime of failure.

At the outset, Mrs. Rice's boarding house allows Judith to feed anew upon her illusions, and it is in this microcosm of Belfast society that she moves from hope through despair to defeat. The net decline in her position is relatively slight, but in an arena where much of the action is below subsistence level and where even holding one's own represents failure, any backsliding at all takes on the proportions of a disaster. Collectively, the inhabitants of this house represent an accumulation of the pettiness, hostility, and prejudice that a parochial society produces; individually, they remain isolated and static, given to clichés and routine, except for Bernard, the anticlerical and pampered son of the landlady, on whom all their hatred focuses. Moore's initial description of him is a memorable one:

He was a horrid-looking fellow. Fat as a pig he was, and his face was the colour of cottage cheese. His collar was unbuttoned and his silk tie was spotted with egg stain. His stomach stuck out like a sagging pillow and his little thin legs fell away under it to end in torn felt slippers. He was all bristly blond jowls, tiny puffy hands and long blond curly hair, like some monstrous baby swelled to man size. (*JH*, 9)

Unlike the other boarders—Miss Friel, Mr. Lenehan, and James Madden—Bernard is not intellectually barren, for in his rational anticlericalism he emerges as the one perceptive critic of his society. "When I devised the character of Bernard Rice," Moore explained, "I gave him some of my own opinions. The ideas about God's omniscience and omnipotence, for example. . . . I had to make him a lapsed Catholic because if he had been a Protestant and a rational anti-clerical sort of person, Miss Hearne would have ignored what he said."[6] He thus represents for Judith a rational escape from religious bonds, and in his lechery he also constitutes a potential sexual release, two remedies that she desperately needs. But that Moore uses Bernard to represent an alternative both to the institutionalized religion and to the enforced chastity of Belfast society constitutes a severe measure of that society indeed, and it poignantly dramatizes the seriousness of Judith's plight.

Judith's relationship with James Madden is the more central one, and it reflects the urgency of her need to acquire a social and a sexual status. Her spiritual needs, after all, like those of the community at large, can be adequately fulfilled by her Sunday-morning routines; it is only when her identity as a social and sexual being becomes unrealizable that she dares go beyond the clichés of her religious teachings. So Madden offers what at first appears to be a miraculous opportunity: unlike all other males in her life, he does not immediately reject her, and his seeming dependence on her, his taking her out socially, and his experiences in the larger world all feed her fantasies and give her renewed hope. One of the narrative strengths of this novel is the way Moore manipulates these two protagonists, whose actions toward one another are initially fed by hope, illusion, and deceit, and whose gradual and inevitable disillusionment means in effect the end of both their schemes.

Madden is a version of a frequently recurring figure in Moore's fiction, the failed Irishman, the most lonely of all of Moore's exiles, whom we meet later in such characters as Billy Davis in *Ginger Coffey* or Turlough Carnahan in "Uncle T," and, indeed, in Ginger himself. Like Judith, but for different reasons, Madden too is rejected by his Belfast society; he threatens Bernard's pampered position, he challenges Lenehan's complacency, and for his fellow pubsters he is merely a "Yankee walking free drink concession." Moore makes an implicit social comment here: this rejection stems not from any moral or intellectual superiority on either side, but from the ingrained fears and jealousies that characterize Moore's Belfastians. It is appropriate that in this theater of hostility and rejection Moore should establish a confrontation between two rejects whose frustrations and designs upon one another unite them temporarily into a tenuous and desperate league.

Nevertheless, for the moment Madden constitutes for Judith the possibility of a future that accords her both social and sexual fulfillment, possibilities that begin increasingly to constitute her reawakened fantasies. Up to that point she had characteristically bolstered her status by resurrecting her past, and indeed, her only explanation to Mrs. Rice about her family· is that their "very interesting history" derives from the fact that "they're all buried out in Nun's Bush . . . , one of the oldest cemeteries in the country" (*JH*, 11). The past of course remains operative: Judith's fantasies about Madden and her rejection of him when she discovers he was only a doorman derive in large part from the residual influence of her long-dead Aunt D'Arcy. In that climactic seventh chapter, Judith rationalizes valiantly, if pitifully, between the twin illusions of past and future, and in effect rejects both by choosing the present moment and its only solution, her secret cache of whiskey. Psychologically and aesthetically, the scene of reminiscence which follows this surrender is convincing, for it is only in a state of intoxication—that is, of unreality—that Judith is able to face the reality of her dilemma:

A drink would put things right. Drink was not to help forget, but to help remember, to clarify and arrange untidy and unpleasant facts into a perfect pattern of reasonableness and beauty. Alcoholic, she did not drink to put aside the dangers and disappointments of the moment. She drank to be able to see these trials more philosophically, to examine them more fully, fortified by the stimulant of unreason. (*JH*, 106-107)

Judith's progress from final hope to final relapse is played out within a world that is essentially lifeless and hostile, a fact she is reminded of wherever she turns. The boarding house itself "was silent, a house in mid-morning when all the world is out at work" (*JH*, 30), the empty parish church was "cleared of its stock of rituals, invocations, prayers, a deserted spiritual warehouse" (*JH*, 121), and, indeed, the entire city of Belfast proclaimed its barrenness for Judith:

There, under the great dome of the building, ringed around by forgotten memorials, bordered by the garrison neatness of a Garden of Remembrance, everything that was Belfast came into focus. The newsvendors calling out the great events of the world in flat, uninterested Ulster voices; the drab facades of the buildings grouped around the Square, proclaiming the virtues of trade, hard dealing and Presbyterian righteousness. The order, the neatness, the floodlit cenotaph, a white respectable phallus planted in stinking Irish bog. The Protestant dearth of gaiety, the Protestant surfeit of order, the dour Ulster burghers walking proudly among the monuments to their mediocrity. (*JH*, 90)

Appropriately, it is here, in "the designated centre of the city" that Judith waits "for a word," for the transformation of Madden's hints into the substance of romance, "something that might lead to something wonderful" (*JH*, 90). But the only word she gets is the blunt word of reality, which has the effect, when Judith sees her only other alternative, of finally making her face reality for the first time. "That's what I've come to," she confesses to Moira O'Neill later. "Turned down by a doorman. And what's more, I didn't want to be turned down. I'd take him yet" (*JH*, 200).

Though Judith in all these personal crises is very much a victim of her own sexual frustrations and of her impulsive behavior, she is also a victim of a code of absolute morality and of a repressive, Calvinistic religious order which administers punishment rather than compassion. These two planes of conflict, Judith's human desire to fulfill herself sexually and socially, and the dehumanized institutional forces within Belfast which militate against this tendency, are skillfully juxtaposed by Moore and allow us to see in dramatic form just what it means to be a victim of a pervasive determinism. As mentioned earlier, Judith not infrequently contributes to her own destruction by her uncritical acceptance of the social and religious pronouncements of her society, and as John Wilson Foster quite rightly points out, the novel's central irony resides in the fact that Judith "suffers for her sexual deprivation precisely in proportion to her piety."[7] Her attitudes toward the Church vary according to the nature of her crises and range from childlike submission to savage attack, from the comfort of clichés to the agony of unanswerable questions.

Though Judith all her life has derived consolation from the rituals of the Church, she has by novel's end, though without realizing it, essentially adopted the anticlerical position defined by Bernard in his violent outburst to her:

Religion is it? And what has religion ever done for you, may I ask? Do you think God gives a damn about the likes of you and me? I don't know what got you into this mess . . . but I know what's keeping you this way. Your silly religious scruples. You're waiting for a miracle. Look at yourself: a poor piano teacher, lonely, drinking yourself crazy in a furnished room. Do you want to thank God for that? (*JH*, 159)

For the first time in her life, she is sufficiently shaken to go to the priest for genuine answers rather than for stock responses; when she

poses for him the very substance of the Christian purpose in one
frenzied question: "Do you understand? *Do you understand?*" he is
rendered helpless in all three of his traditional roles:

Shepherd, he looked at his sheep. What ails her? Father, he did not
comprehend what his child was saying. Priest, he could not communicate
with his parishioner. "No," Father Quigley said. "I don't know what you're
talking about." (*JH*, 206)

Father Quigley's rejection of her here not only constitutes the
ultimate betrayal of the very foundations of Judith's existence, but
together with Madden's earlier sexual betrayal and the social
betrayal perpetrated by the boarding house inhabitants, deprives
her of her last possibilities for fulfillment. Within this perspective,
her melodramatic attack upon the tabernacle dramatizes the release
of all her pent-up tensions that had accumulated during her years of
waiting, years during which her avoidance of any direct confrontation with experience allowed her fantasies to sustain her. Deprived
simultaneously of her possibilities and her fantasies alike, Judith
must therefore remove herself from the world which both engen-
dered and destroyed these two psychological supports, and from this
perspective, Earnscliffe House becomes more than merely another
stopover in her decline: it becomes the final one, where she can
nurture her illusions without ever having to test them again.

In its depiction of how a society can destroy a character, *Judith
Hearne* is as close to a naturalistic novel as Moore ever comes, and
he is never again to exploit so consistently the drearier aspects of life
common to such novels. But in his social analysis he is, like Henry
James or George Eliot, a moral realist rather than a scientific
determinist, and indeed, Eliot's famous injunction in *Adam Bede*
could well constitute Moore's own position here:

These fellow-mortals, everyone, must be accepted as they are: you can
neither straighten their noses, nor brighten their wit, nor rectify their
dispositions; and it is these people . . . that it is needful you should tolerate,
pity, and love: it is these more or less ugly, stupid, inconsistent people . . .
for whom you should cherish all possible hopes, all possible patience.[8]

III   The Feast of Lupercal (1957)[9]

The determinism which operates in the second of Moore's Belfast
novels derives, as in *Judith Hearne*, from a complex of forces, but in

a sense it is even more depressing in its effect, in that it defeats an individual with much more going for him than Judith had. Like Judith, Diarmuid Devine is lonely, unmarried, and virgin, but unlike her he has a number of qualities and talents that normally should be sufficient: he is a competent English teacher and drama coach, he is generally accepted and well liked within Belfast's social world, and he can satisfactorily explain and accept his single state without having to indulge in alcoholic or other illusory rationalizations. He is aware of what his problems and shortcomings are, and knows what he must do to achieve moral and psychological independence, but so thoroughly has he been conditioned during his thirty-seven years that he cannot act when his moment comes; when he does make a desperate and belated move, the system both protects and defeats him by compelling him to accept with even more finality his former stance of acquiescent conformity.

In *Judith Hearne*, Moore had dramatized the aftermath of failure; in *Lupercal* it is the moment of failure that constitues the dramatic center, and because we are with Dev when he chooses it, our responses to him are quite different from what they were toward Judith. Because she lacked those qualities and powers of introspection which are necessary for even a minimal success, she would likely have failed in any society, no matter how flexible and benign, and thus for her we express primarily an overwhelming sense of pity. For Dev, on the other hand, our pity is mixed with impatience, for we see him several times on the point of asserting himself and are pulling for him because his failure is not preordained as Judith's was. "I feel equal sympathy with this hero," Moore said in a letter to Mordecai Richler after the novel was published, "but the cards are not stacked against him so much. He has more free choices and therefore it is harder to be compassionate with him. But this situation, I think, corresponds more to real life than did the [Judith Hearne] one—in that the hero *has* a choice."[10]

We are made aware of these weaknesses in Dev's makeup throughout the novel, most characteristically through patterns which demonstrate the conflicts between his social and his psychological self. Indeed, the novel opens with a clear announcement of his social being: "DIARMUID DEVINE, B.A. (Junior and Senior English)," but we soon detect an inconsistency about him: "He was a tall man, yet did not seem so: not youthful, yet somehow young; a man whose appearance suggested some painful uncertainty. . . . The military bravura of his large mustache was denied by weak eyes, circled by ill-fitting spectacles" (*FL*, 6). Neither completely the conformist nor completely the individual, he is, like Eliot's Prufrock, whom interestingly he resembles in a number of ways, vaguely aware that he would like to "disturb the universe," but his "do I dare" never really gets beyond an inchoate articulation; indeed, as with Macbeth, that other procrastinator evoked by this novel, Dev's "I would" and his "I dare not" "wait upon" each other, as it were, to produce a paralysis of will. By novel's end, he becomes totally aware of what his problem really is, and his confession that "to fail to sin, perhaps that is my sin" (*FL*, 218) simply confirms that, in the ordinary routine of his life, it has been, to modify Lady Macbeth's observation, the deed and not the thought which has confounded him. Unlike Judith and the later Ginger Coffey, however, Dev is never deluded by his deficiencies, and he continually experiences mortification because of his habit of honest introspection, and because his social self always dictates self-conscious retreat rather than assertion. "We're completely different types," the betrayed Una sums up. "I want to fight against what life's doing to me, and you're afraid to. Live and let live is your motto" (*FL*, 192).

In both form and content, *Lupercal* is Moore's most realistic novel, avoiding both the subjective overtones of his first one and the formal experimentations of many of his later works. Though there are some modifications of the prevailing third-person point of view and, as in *Judith Hearne*, a few oblique shots of the protagonist through the eyes of some minor characters, our comprehension of Dev and our compassion for him derive essentially from the precise and orderly fashion with which Moore dramatizes his dilemma and prepares us for the inevitability of his failure. As in *Judith Hearne*, the basic technique involves a modified slice-of-life approach, for Saint Michan's College (Ardath College in the English edition) constitutes as convincing a microcosm of Belfast society in *Lupercal* as the Rice boarding house did in the earlier novel. As the novel unfolds, Saint Michan's emerges as both a literal and a symbolic representation of the determinism which pervades the world that Dev inhabits: its insistence upon order and blind obedience to its day-to-day routines and its extended influence within the isolated enclaves of Belfast's social life shape virtually every move that Dev makes. And within Saint Michan's, Dev as a lay master is an agent of the authority it wields, but as its former student he is also a lingering victim of that authority, and the suspension that Moore creates between these two tendencies in Dev constitutes one of *Lupercal*'s major strengths.

Saint Michan's was very closely modeled upon the Jesuit Saint Malachy's College that Moore himself attended, his recollections of which remain unpleasantly etched in his memory. "The system of education described in [*Lupercal*]," he stated in a letter to his publisher in 1956, "is still the way most Irish Catholics are untaught in everything save cowardice, conformity and cruelty. This is, I feel, Ireland today—a place which has nothing in common with the stories of Frank O'Connor . . . and all the other old brogue writers, who, as *croyants*, always did subordinate their art to the demands of their faith."[11] The authorities obviously felt that Moore subordinated nothing in his depiction of Catholic education, for *Lupercal* was promptly banned in Ireland, though such are the vicissitudes of art and morality even in that repressed country that it later became required reading in some Irish schools. At any rate, Moore's honest realism here produced a convincing analysis not only of a specific Jesuit institution of education, but, more importantly, of its stultifying effect upon individuals involved in it and concomitantly upon an entire nation. "I feel Devine's moral cowardice," he confessed to his publisher, "is in some degree the condition of all Irishmen today. Self government did not bring them freedom of thought."

As an external, precipitating agent responsible for Devine's abortive rebellion against the closed world, Una Clarke represents values and possibilities that he has never allowed himself to entertain except in fantasy. On the surface there appears to be little chance of a serious relationship developing between them, for the factors which separate them represent the major sociological, religious, and moral issues which divide Ireland: his Belfast background against her Dublin upbringing, his Catholicism against her Protestantism, his sexual repression against her seeming paganism, and his servitude against her emancipation. In short, everything that Una represents violates the letter and the spirit of the narrow, authoritarian code that has shaped Dev's responses to the world. Yet a strong mutual attraction does develop between them, although, as with Judith and Madden, the elements of rejection and desperation initially play their part, and Dev soon finds himself confronting fundamental issues he has never before had any need to examine.

The culmination of this relationship ironically involves a testing of the rumor and innuendo which precipitated it in the first place. Dev has carefully prepared his social and outward self in order to achieve his long-deprived sexual identity: his new clothes and his frenzied dancing lessons which overcame his earlier "mathematical shuffle and multiplying feet" helped make him an acceptable alternative to her Dublin betrayer, and even Belfast's closed-up premises conspired to drive them into the privacy of his digs. The ensuing escapade surely constitutes one of the most convincing, comic-pathetic seduction scenes in contemporary fiction, and, ironically, all it serves to do is to establish the inevitability of their severance. For by remaining chaste and thus disproving the rumors about her reputation, Una votes herself out of a world whose terms are dictated by its Moloneys: a Protestant girl from Dublin who is not promiscuous violates too many prejudices to be allowed to remain. Dev, on the other hand, sinks more deeply into his world, for by substantiating the rumors about his sexual innocence and incompetence, he puts himself in a position where it will be more difficult than ever to challenge opinions about other manifestations of his basic inadequacies.

Devine knows that the causes of his shortcomings are not solely internal, for they derive in no small part from a social and educational system that breeds ignorance rather than sophistication. "As for girls," he muses at the outset, "well, he had never been a ladies' man. He was not ugly, no, nor too shy, no, but he never had much luck with girls. It was the education in Ireland, dammit, he had said it many a time. . . . Saint Michan's cared little for appearances or social graces" (*FL*, 9). In many respects, Devine represents the hypothetical Irish bachelor, who is in no rush to get married. He is cautious and unromantic, quite unprepared to risk his reputation and security for the possibilities inherent in new experiences. Fear of change, fear of upsetting anyone, fear of social disapproval— these are Dev's besetting problems, and the fact that he knows he has them makes him something of a tragic rather than merely a pathetic character. Ultimately, Dev and Una represent more than just Catholic versus Protestant; they stand for two diametrically opposed views of life which, under the conditions which exist in their world, are finally incompatible.

Moore's implied thesis here is supported by sociological studies of sex and marriage in Ireland, and particularly revealing is a study entitled *The Vanishing Irish*,[12] published at about the same time that Moore began writing his Belfast novels. The statistics in this document are revealing—the lowest marriage rate in the civilized world, the highest proportion of unmarried males in the world, and

the oldest average marriage age in the world—but more disturbing
yet is the attitude of the Irish toward the whole question. "The
average man does not regard the prospects of matrimony seriously
until he has reached his thirties," notes one of the contributors.
"Then too often he finds himself in a groove, a fixed mode of
existence, which he is loath to abandon. . . ."[13] In large part, this
attitude stems from the indoctrinations of puritanical religion and
educational systems, which foster suspicion, fear and ignorance
toward any matters pertaining to sex. Sean O'Faolain notes that
"the whole question of sex in Ireland is dominated . . . by profound
psychological repressions," and he quotes a letter which could quite
easily have been written by Devine himself:

We Irishmen have been conditioned into a state of sexual frigidity and
repression because for generations we have clothed the sublimity of love in
shrouds of taboo, false prudery and an attitude of Victorian Puritanism that
has given to the act of sexual union the blasphemous nature of something
offensive.[14]

The Vanishing Irish clearly illustrates the causes of the sexual
inadequacies and frustrations which lie at the heart of The Feast of
Lupercal, for in an alarming number of respects Dev is a composite
of the traits of the Irish bachelor figure castigated by many of the
contributors to this document. In light of its sociological revelations,
both Una and Dev make predictable responses to their dilemmas,
and Lupercal's lack of sentimentality and melodrama testifies to the
faithfulness with which Moore's realism in this novel reflects the
world that he obviously had carefully observed. As a microcosm of
this world, Saint Michan's provides a credible framework in which
Moore can use both its inmates and its routines to underscore the
relationship between a Puritanical authority and the curse of sterility
which besets all of Ireland.

The determinism which informs Lupercal can quite profitably be
viewed as a manifestation of the roles played by the various
individuals responsible for administering the secular and spiritual
authority invested in Saint Michan's, particularly by the two at the
extremes of its hierarchy, who, by the nature of their duties, are also
the most detached from the human dilemmas within the institution.
The mechanical routine of the school is controlled by the deaf
custodian, John Harbinson, whose ritual of bell-ringing routinely
announces to school and community alike the pervasiveness of a
rigid order:

At that moment, in a small cubbyhole off the entrance hall of Saint Michan's College, the hall porter pushed a key into the switch block and pressed it down. An electric bell, deafeningly loud, screamed out into corridors, crying unheard in empty dormitories, echoing across wet playing fields to die in the faraway mists over Belfast Lough. (*FL*, 3)

Significantly, the faculty telephone at Saint Michan's—the means of communicating with the outside world—is located next to this bell mechanism, as Dev is sternly reminded when he receives, in violation of regulations, a phone call from Una. "Sorry about the bell," old Harbinson tells Dev. "But I have my orders, sir, nothing must interfere with the bell" (*FL*, 77). Appropriately, the custodian is virtually deaf, so while he can talk to the inhabitants of Saint Michan's, they cannot communicate with him: he is the perfect agent of a blind, authoritarian order.

At the other extreme of the school's hierarchy, the venerable director of this order rules his world with a cunning and a firmness that belie his apparent doddering ineffectuality. Remote from colleagues and students alike, the Very Reverend Daniel Keogh depends almost exclusively on old Harbinson to provide him with every vestige of rumor or scandal that could threaten his authority. He stands beyond the vagaries of human passion, and unlike the Father Abbot of *Catholics*, he appears to be impervious to doubt or to indecision, treating with the same degree of finality both Devine's moral predicament and Father McSwiney's scheming political ploy. Keogh emerges as the tyrannical Jesuit figure who will stop at nothing if his universe is threatened; while he reacts with dignity and ostensibly with compassion, he in fact is ruthless and Machiavellian, a point Moore elaborated on some years ago:

The headmaster, [whom] many critics mistakenly took for a kind old man, is to my mind the very spirit of authoritarianism and Catholicism at its worst. He is *Realpolitik* all the way. He doesn't give a damn for anything but the good of the school. He is the person I think one should be frightened of.[15]

A measure of Devine's limitations was that he in fact did not sufficiently understand the nature of Keogh's "kindness" to be afraid of him. By succumbing to his importuning on behalf of outward harmony, Dev effectively sacrificed his private self and any further chance of emancipation to the demands of his social world.

Ironically, it is Saint Michan's itself which precipitates Dev's rebellion in the first place, for it is the gossip he overhears about himself in the jakes that leads to his initial liaison with Una. But having opened up this possibility for him, it denies him its fruition, and it governs every aspect of the ensuing relationship, either by direct interference, as with the school play, or, more insidiously, through its undercurrents of gossip and innuendo which permeate every level of the school. Within the staff and student body of Saint Michan's, too, the various intrigues, rivalries, and betrayals reflect the hostile nature of this world and conspire to perpetuate Dev's own timidity, indecision, and fear of social disapproval. For him there is at the resolution of his abortive rebellion only a sinking back into the sterile and stultifying world from which he might have emerged; for Una there is the more tolerant and expansive world of London, for in spite of Dev's last-minute confessions she is ultimately unable to accept his surrender to his own mediocrity.

The symbolic and literal planes of this novel come together in an interesting and skillful fashion in the various manipulations of its Lupercalian theme. Devine's caning of his students is, on the level of the novel's realism, simply the order of the day at Saint Michan's, with masters and students alike accepting both its inevitability and its corrective potential. But it is also symbolically for Dev a means of self-flagellation to atone not only for his sexual barrenness, but for his moral and psychological limitations as well. As his deepening affair with Una increasingly brings him closer to making a sexual and moral commitment, he is goaded both by his own fears of his inadequacies and by the taunts of his students to intensify his canings until that final day of his rebellion when, "in a terrible wax," he lashes out indiscriminately on the slightest pretext. In an ironic reversal of the Roman fertility rite, here it is the barren Dev who flogs the innocent boys; his explanation to them of the Lupercalian ritual ironically constitutes the solution that he himself must seek in order to achieve atonement, but his desperate rationale that "that question is sometimes asked by the examiners" (*FL*, 216) simply underscores how incapable he is at this moment of chaos of seeing the real nature of his problem.

It is only in his later solitude on the playing field that he is able to come to a clear moral decision about his inadequacies: "Keeping quiet, being afraid to own up, that was the real sin" (*FL*, 218). At this point, all the beatings he had administered, and the real significance of the Lupercalia, coalesce to enable him, like Ginger Coffey and Brendan Tierney, to say "*My fault*," and make a full

confession to Una's uncle about his responsibility for her dilemma.
Thus Dev achieves momentarily a full moral victory, but, as with
his other achievements in his life, there is no one to share his
triumph with him; Heron, as the victim of this sudden and
uncharacteristic display of truth, can only respond in a fit of
irrational and uncontrollable violence, and the Lupercalian theme
takes yet another turn. The normal Lupercalian ceremony where
whippings were administered to bestow fertility is here rendered
superfluous, for Dev has already achieved his fertility, as it were,
before being caned; the whippings administered to him are in effect
the outward manifestations of his own self-flagellations that he has
experienced for his cowardice and his betrayals. "It's a form of
expiation," he later explains to Una (*FL*, 244), and the fact that she
doesn't understand what he means indicates that for the first and
only time in their relationship he gains a moral victory over her, and
underscores again their essential incompatibility.

As has been shown, the two planes of Dev's identity, the social
and the personal, have been in operation throughout *Lupercal;* and
though he in a very real sense sacrifices his individuality for the sake
of social harmony, it is significant that it is a personal and not a
social impulse that controls his final act. It was not society's
condemnation of the attempted seduction scene and its aftermath
which caused Una and Dev to go their separate ways, but a mutual
and individual recognition of their basic incompatibility. Dev's
decision not to meet her at the station reflects his acceptance of the
way his nature has been conditioned toward conformity: "She was
right, he couldn't change. For the rest of his life he'd go on telling
people what they wanted to hear" (*FL*, 246). Like the "harnessed,
dumb" horse that stands obediently, "looking wildly down the
avenue in the narrow focus of its blinkers" (*FL*, 246), Dev may also
experience a kind of vestigial impulse here, but, as Judith Hearne
discovered, there is really no escape from a lifetime of conditioning
or from an environment of suppression.

IV The Emperor of Ice-Cream (1965)[16]

Judith Hearne and *The Feast of Lupercal* constitute important
achievements for Moore, and for many readers still rank among the
best novels he has written, and Judith in particular lingers as a
moving and unforgettable character. He has never since, however,
turned to such unrelievedly bleak subject matter or stuck so closely
to a realistic style, and even as he finished those first novels, he

communicated to one of his editors his sense of having reached an aesthetic impasse:

> I always want to give my character more diversity, more intellectual strength—something of that wonderful Dostoevskian quality of the unexpected, which, on examination turns out to be the logical, the underlying truth in their behavior. But, so far, each time I simply lack the ability to bring this off and lacking it, settle for what my pessimism and my experience tell me is possible. So the characters become smaller, duller in a way and without the stature of tragedy. . . . [Each] of these books is a failure in terms of what I would have liked to do with them at the beginning, but . . . their development seemed to be forced on me by some pessimistic sense of truth about human behaviour. This, I know, is a failure of my imagination and leaves me dissatisfied in the end.[17]

There is a refreshing honesty—and not a little modesty—in this confession, but it is nonetheless true that it is really only in these first two novels that Moore fairly closely repeats himself. He is to turn to Belfast again for his material in later novels, but he never again conveys such a despairing vision of experience; and in his subsequent works he moves increasingly away from a realistic approach toward more flexible and experimental modes.

In retrospect, even more so than *The Emperor of Ice-Cream*, both *Judith Hearne* and *The Feast of Lupercal* emerge as obligatory novels, wherein Moore purged himself of the bitterness he felt toward Belfast. In a sense he was an angry young man in those days, but unlike many of his counterparts in Britain he rarely allowed his anger to override his compassion. At that stage of his writing, his personal experiences and observations in a very real sense dictated his aesthetic approach, with the realistic novel emerging for him as the most appropriate vehicle to communicate the blend of social analysis and personal outrage he directed toward Belfast from his North American vantage point. But at the same time, his New World experiences were steadily serving to modify both his metaphysics and his aesthetics, and increasingly the comic mode and other manifestations of an antirealistic stance began to characterize his fiction. Within this perspective, though Moore was to turn again to his recollections of Belfast for important backdrops to such later novels as *Fergus* and *The Doctor's Wife*, *The Emperor of Ice-Cream* marks the culmination of his concern with that city as an exclusive shaping force on character. If in *Judith Hearne* he used this backdrop to dramatize the aftermath of failure, and in *Lupercal* the moment of failure, then in *Emperor* he uses it to examine the prerequisites of failure before the individual is doomed to defeat.

Gavin Burke, at seventeen, is both Moore's youngest protagonist and according to his own admission his most autobiographical one, but the fact that he waited until his fifth novel to write his *Bildungsroman* allowed him to apply a chronological and aesthetic distancing to offset the risk of pure autobiography. Moore's use of a twenty-five-year-old event to illuminate Gavin's situation is both historically accurate and aesthetically convincing: the bombing of Belfast suddenly made manifest the supremacy of the *carpe diem* philosophy which Gavin's fumbling rebellion against the confining forces of that dead city had already anticipated. A product of the same school and the same religious forces that shaped Devine, and both seemingly immobilized by the priority of their fantasy life over reality, Gavin becomes an accidental beneficiary of history, while Dev remains its rationalizing victim. Throughout his fiction, Moore consistently demonstrates his thesis that an inward-looking, Calvinistic world like Belfast does not readily release its victims; *Emperor* reveals this possibility through an external, almost cosmic, intervention coinciding with the right moment in someone's life, while a novel like *The Doctor's Wife* dramatizes how such a moment can be transformed by a deliberate and self-serving courage.

Gavin's situation, among other things, reflects the recurring son-father conflict that characterizes much of Moore's fiction and which finds at least a temporary resolution both in this novel and in *The Mangan Inheritance*. It is particularized here in the successful rebellion that Gavin wages against his father and the values he stands for, significantly during a period in history when the world in a sense was held in temporary suspension. Symbolically, the phony war goes beyond the mere absence of military confrontation: it suggests a questioning of the very values which the war was presumably going to preserve. During this period, Gavin's ARP duties appear to be both absurd and unproductive, and he fluctuates between his father's world and his own, "one dead and the other powerless to be born," so to speak. The bombing of Belfast not only suddenly transforms his ARP exercises into productive actions but indicates that nothing less than a total destruction of his father's world will suffice; the final meeting of Gavin and his father in their empty house, now significantly "condemned," becomes in this perspective a most effective resolution.

When the novel opens, however, Gavin faces a recurring moral crisis brought on by his academic failures, his sexual frustrations, and his spiritual misgivings, a crisis which assumes a traditional Morality format:

He had two guardian angels. The White Angel sat on his right shoulder and advised the decent thing. The Black Angel sat on his left shoulder and pleaded the devil's cause. The White Angel was the official angel: everybody had one. It had all been explained to him in catechism class when he was a little boy. In catechism class the Black Angel was barely mentioned. Yet, the trouble was, the Black Angel seemed more intelligent; more his sort. (*EIC*, 10)

In his incipient rebellion, coming to the aid of his White Angel are virtually his entire family, his off-and-on sweetheart, Sally Shannon, and his Divine Infant of Prague, "a desperate little preacher whose aim in life was to catch Gavin Burke's eye" (*EIC*, 3). In support of himself, aside from his Black Angel, he has only his sister, Kathy, and his own inchoate conviction that somehow he is on the right track. Opposed to his family's obsession with the traditional goals of education, security, and success, and their operating principle of expediency, Gavin opts for a vision of the future spelled out by such poets as Auden, MacNeice, and Yeats, a vision which predicates a New World built on the ruins of the Old:

Yeats knew what nonsense it was, in this day and age, to talk of futures and jobs. But how could you explain that to Owen, who had read nothing for pleasure since his *Boys' Own Weekly* days? How could you tell him that, for you, the war was an event which had produced in you a shameful secret excitement, a vision of the grownups' world in ruins? It would not matter in that ruined world if Gavin Burke had failed his Schools Leaving Certificate. The records would be buried in rubble. War was freedom, freedom from futures. There was nothing in the world so imposing that a big bomb couldn't blow it up. (*EIC*, 7)

Gavin's first step toward the realization of his goal is to isolate himself from the world of conventional Belfast, and, as Ginger Coffey discovered, his descent to the bottom compelled him to see the reality of his world in a different light. At the very least, his joining the ARP constitutes a protest against the rabid nationalism of his Aunt Liz, "a heavily mustached widow who wore unchanging black in memory of Gavin's uncle, killed twenty years before in the Irish Troubles" (*EIC*, 11). For Gavin, her preoccupation with a dead issue and unwillingness to acknowledge the priority of current crises take on a frightening irrelevancy in a world where "We shall go down like palaeolithic man/Before some new Ice Age or Genghiz Khan" (*EIC*, 7). But in addition, his association with the bizarre group of misfits in the ARP allows him, with a newly discovered and somewhat bewildering sense of the amorality of things, to effect more closely a conjunction of his fantasy world and the real world. Though he does not, as he prophesies, "go out and buy [himself] great scarlet whores," he does participate in the occasional bout of drunkenness and teeters on the edge of sexual conquests and homosexuality, experiences that, as he mused, represented "a grown-up world, undreamed of in the St. Michan's school philosophy" (*EIC*, 97).

Unlike Mrs. Rice's boarding house in *Judith Hearne* or Saint Michan's in *Lupercal*, post officer Craig's ARP unit does not properly constitute a microcosm of Belfast society; rather, like the group of proofreaders in *Ginger Coffey*, it represents an absurd extension of the normal world, where behavior patterns and tendencies are distorted out of their reality. Craig, a sadistic and stupid man, whose "pale skin glistened like a newly peeled potato" (*EIC*, 13), is only slightly more eccentric than the rest of his group, "an old soldier who dyes his hair black, a drunken officer type, a hod carrier, a dwarf, some old charladies, and a blonde semi-whore" (*EIC*, 36). Neither collectively nor individually do these individuals pose any threat for Gavin, in the way that Judith and Dev were threatened by their segment of the world: the group's approval or disapproval of Gavin really had no significance or import, since it remained merely as an absurd appendage of the real world until the bombs began to fall, at which point it became the real world, with Gavin in command. Judith's and Dev's groups, on the other hand, were permanent sectors of the real life in which they were compelled to operate forever, and approval or disapproval for them had very tangible consequences.

The realistically depicted sociological world of *Judith Hearne* and *Lupercal* is only occasionally visible in *Emperor*, for Moore's aesthetic concern here takes him generally away from the requirements of literal realism. Yet on Gavin's initial reporting to the Crummick Street First Aid Post, we are given a vivid picture of the sectarian, social, and domestic realities of this world, a scene which evokes Joyce's "Counterparts":

The house was small, the corner house in a row of red-brick workingmen's dwellings in a street sown with children who played chalk games on the pavements, wound ropes around street lamps to make Maypoles, and scrawled NO POPE HERE and UP THE PRODS in its narrow back entries. It was a street to which cloth-capped, collarless men returned heavy with porter when the pubs shut, a street in which husbands slapped pinafored wives, wives slapped small children, and grandmothers screamed imprecations at grandfathers who urinated too near the weekly wash in the back yard. (*EIC*, 12)

The drinking, the beatings, the imprecations, and the screaming evoked by this slice-of-life scene are to have their absurdly harmless counterparts in Gavin's ensuing ARP experiences, but, as is appropriate to the ongoing ascendancy of his fantasy life, he rarely speculates on the real significance of these experiences. Even his continuing association with the Socialist Freddy Hargreaves, whose appreciation of the modern poets created an immediate and lasting bond between them, leads to nothing more serious than participating in left-wing plays and mooching off vulgar capitalist acquaintances. It is only when the world becomes nonpolitical, and faces destruction from an enemy which unites momentarily all of Belfast, that Gavin and Freddy carry out their most useful acts, and then it is necessity and humanity which move them, and not politics.

In Gavin's desire to overcome the two main forces in the real world that frustrate him, his father's code of hard work and success and his girl friend's code of sexual purity, the ARP interlude offers in effect opportunity without consequences. Post officer Craig replaces Gavin's father as the figure of authority, and Gavin not only can ridicule and challenge him with impunity, but can agree to participate in a plot to assassinate him—an abortive plan, as it turns out, but nevertheless in his fantasy a total triumph over a figure of tyranny. The eager girls in the theater and dance halls, and in particular the excitingly available Sheila Luddin, become substitutes for the virtuous Sally Shannon, and it was Gavin's drunkenness which incapacitated him on one of these occasions, and not any moral qualms about the sexual act iself. Thus, external and internal forces alike operate to preserve Gavin's innocence, and his first view both of corpses and nude women ironically coincides with his sudden and grim task of coffining bodies; it is this existential experience, too, that allows him to achieve his triumph over both his father and Sally.

The Sally-Sheila polarity reflects the essential sexual dilemma that Gavin experiences, and that he escapes both of them suggests the more substantial maturity that he ultimately achieves. On one level Sheila of course constitutes the sudden coming to life of the totality of Gavin's lascivious thoughts he had all along entertained about Sally: she is the "great scarlet whore" he had frequently fantasized. That he does not succeed in seducing her is on the literal level due to his intoxication: Shakespeare long ago spoke accurate words about the relationship among drink, desire, and performance. But symbolically, his failure reflects the ambivalence of his feelings toward Sally: on the one hand he wants to ravish her, but on the other he wants, like Salinger's Holden Caulfield, to see purity prevail. At a crucial point in the novel, his fears about his role in the assassination plot overcome his rebellion, and for the moment he succumbs almost ecstatically to this version of purity:

It was like confession in the days when he had believed in confession. . . . There was a great joy, a sense of your burdens being lifted. . . . Sally was right, he could reform if she helped him. They would go out together . . . and theirs would be real love, nothing to do with the dirty sex thoughts which teemed in his mind, but real love, pure love. Then, later on, they would marry and have a family. . . . O God, it was such a relief to give in, to be welcomed back. (*EIC*, 139)

The ensuing reality in bombed-out Belfast, however, destroys this vision, for Sally's refusal to kiss the exhausted Gavin in front of a doctor seems to verify his earlier assessment of her, that she is "a little Catholic bourgeois prig whose main interest in life seems to be the rules of courting etiquette" (*EIC*, 55). Though Gavin concludes his sexual quest as chaste as when he started, he has, like Dana Hilliot of Malcolm Lowry's *Ultramarine*, accumulated both the degree of experience and the appropriate vision to recognize that the urgency of sexual initiation has been replaced by its inevitability in the course of time. And just as Hilliot rejected his girl, Janet, who still confuses innocence with "the sun shining ever so brightly" and grass looking "wonderfully fresh after the rain,"[18] so Gavin dismisses Sally, who, he realizes, is still "somewhere between the world of school and the world of grownups" (*EIC*, 160).

From this perspective, it can be seen that Gavin's sexual problems constitute a relatively minor aspect of a much more complex mission: his attainment of psychological maturity against the formidable opposition of the forces which opposed that, particularly his family and the Church. As reflected in the two earlier Belfast novels, these two institutions characteristically tried to keep their subjects in a state of childlike dependency, and *Emperor* is no exception to this tendency. There is here, however, the added comic dimension: Gavin *is* a child as the novel opens, and the discrepancy, for example, between his sexual fantasy of "himself, wearing his steel helmet, dashing into the house across the way" to rescue the half-naked typist, and the reality of his "battle-dress pants . . . tripping him" (*EIC*, 8) arouses a vastly different response than did our contemplation of Dev's rational justification of his virginal state. In a very real sense, Dev has nothing stopping him except his imagination, whereas for Gavin everything conspires to stop him, but nothing can tame his imagination.

It is appropriate that the opening scenes, where Gavin is just beginning to give full flight to his fantasies, and the closing scenes, where he has attained his maturity, are both enacted in his parents' sitting room, a room in which, as Gavin muses on both occasions, "he had acted and reacted, had left his mark, and had, in turn, been marked " (*EIC*, 9, 248). It is the room in which he is to be subjected to his father's prejudices and self-righteous preachings, his mother's reproachful silences and pious clichés, his aunt's rabid nationalism—all the manifestations, in short, of the narrow code of thinking and living fostered by Calvinistic Belfast. It is a fine example of Moore's sense of irony here that this phase of Gavin's quest culminates in the Christmas-dinner scene in which—in sharp contrast to the raging political controversy which marks the Dedalus Christmas dinner in Joyce's *Portrait*—nothing more portentous is discussed than the plans for the annual Old Boys' Dance. But it is also the room in which Gavin for the first time sees fear in his father's face as he hears of the bombing of Dublin (appropriately, in the chapter following the Christmas scene), in which in a state of drunkenness he openly defies his father, in which he sees his family preparing to abandon Belfast, and in which, finally, he attains his resolution with his father. "The looking glass room, unchanged since his childhood," Gavin muses at the end, "had changed at last. This house is condemned" (*EIC*, 248).

Gavin's passage from innocence through suffering to this point of deliverance from his father's house is convincing because Moore makes no attempt to enlarge Gavin into heroic proportions. His coming to life among the corpses of Belfast is saved from becoming merely a symbolic tour de force because Gavin is shown as being unaware of any incongruity between the arena of his heroism and his performance; it is the unconscious heroism that Moore communicates here that prevents the scene from lapsing into melodrama or farce. His casual delineation of an adolescent's psychological vacillations is impressive, for the realistic backdrop of historical event never challenges the priority of character; it is as though the reader is living through the period with Gavin, and is momentarily distracted from the real problems of adolescence by the occasional BBC or newspaper report on the war.

One particular scene where historical suspense and psychological possibility are fused into a kind of mythical nexus occurs just after Gavin had failed in yet another sexual assault on Sally upon Cave Hill. In his frustration at his failure, and in his isolation after his dismissal of her, her "Catholic logic," and her Church, in a kind of existential panic he desperately invites his world's destruction:

In the afternoon silence above him, a growl of engines. From a corner of the sky they came, great gray planes of a sort he had never seen before. He stood staring, sure that they were bombers crossing the mountain, bearing down on the city. They roared overhead, rough beasts, their hour come round at last, slouching toward Belfast to be born. Here on the mountainside he would see it all, the explosions, the flames, the holocaust. . . . There they go, groaning over the city in the afternoon sunlight, they must be Germans, they *must* be. (*EIC*, 112)

More than merely a foreshadowing of the eventual bombing, this scene also suggests that Gavin cannot be only a spectator to his world's destruction; the fact, too, that the planes "went out to sea, toward England, toward Europe, far away to that faraway war" dictates the necessity of Gavin's transcending his solipsistic view of the importance of Belfast in his vision of destruction, a point driven home by the Jewish refugee Lili who admonishes Lambert and Gavin for "[hiding] from the war in your little back streets" (*EIC*, 183). Gavin's subsequent drunken escapade with her and a homesick Greek sailor leads directly to his awareness of his expanded consciousness:

But now, perhaps, he *was* becoming a grownup, for, looking back at the bleak St. Michan's days, he saw them in the fond forgetful light of an easier time. Life as an adult could be more terrible than anything a schoolboy might imagine. The Greek of last night danced into his mind, the weeping Greek whose mother, sisters, brothers, might even now be falling under

Nazi guns. He felt sorrow for the Greek, and yet there was a shameful,
guilty comfort in knowing that if he, Gavin Burke, was facing an ominous
future, the rest of the world, whole countries, even, was in the same boat.
(*EIC*, 194)

That very evening, as the bombs began to fall, "within Gavin, there
started an extraordinary elation, a tumult of joy . . . [for] the world
and the war had come to him at last" (*EIC*, 199).

For the first time in Gavin's life, the here and now, not the past or
the future, takes on a crucial significance, and his sudden awareness
that he is able to perform decisively when he has to dissolves all the
doubts and fears which had previously immobilized him. The
bombing thus fulfills two necessary prerequisites to the growth of
Gavin toward psychological maturity: it destroys everything that
measured or dictated his past failure, and it pushes him into a
pragmatic testing of his abilities. "Caught in a cold excitement,
feeling himself witness to history" (*EIC*, 219), he refuses to flee to
Dublin with his family, and his wandering through the collapsing
city from his father's house back to his ARP post takes on a symbolic
significance, representing an initiatory pilgrimage into a new and
unknown world being born out of the ruins of the old. And he is
thus able to stand in silent and unconscious rebellion among a group
of kneeling survivors uttering prayerful thanks with a priest for
being spared:

He could forgive them all, his father, these people, this city, for, after
tonight, nothing they could say or do would hurt him again. There and
then, in the drone of the priest's "but deliver us from evil," he vowed to
deliver himself from the sham of church attendance . . . and compromises
which had helped keep him becalmed in indecision between adolescence
and adult life. Tonight, he felt, at last that he had grown up, escaped. . . .
(*EIC*, 225)

Early in the action of the novel, Gavin had mused over a fragment
of a poem by Wallace Stevens—

> Let be be finale of seem.
> The only emperor is the emperor of ice-cream.

—but had not been quite sure of its meaning, except that "it seemed
to sum things up" (*EIC*, 8). His growth to an understanding of
himself and of his world is paralleled by his gradual and implicit

understanding of these lines, for in the closing scenes of the novel, though he does not articulate their meaning, he is in a very real sense translating them into action: no longer is his "emperor" the authority of the past or the future, but simply the exigencies of the moment. There are other parallels as well, of course. The images of concupiscence and sensual gratification in the first stanza of Stevens's poem find an echo in Gavin's fantasy of buying "great scarlet whores"; and before he is through, he derives a literal appreciation indeed of the cold image of death in the last stanza, as the protruding "horny feet" assume a tangible reality for him in his piecing together and coffining of the corpses. In all these interpretations, however, his "emperor" is the same: it is the overriding priority of the moment, and the realization that everything is in a state of flux.

At any rate, it is interesting to note that Gavin comes into his rebellion on the wings of poetry rather than through any political conviction about the wrongs of the world. And it is not the agonizing and self-pitying "O World! O Life! O Time!" of a Shelley that appeals to him, but the frighteningly concrete details of an impending holocaust spelled out by a group of contemporary poets who "knew the jig was up." It is significant, too, that Moore does not allow Gavin merely to go through the gesture of accepting these poets: his participation in the grim reality of their prediction makes his rebellion much more than a rhetorical flourish.

Gavin's final reconciliation with his father completes the tripartite pattern of rebellion that began with repudiation and moved into isolation, a pattern that is evident as well in Moore's other comic novel, *Ginger Coffey*. In taking his father's hand, Gavin acknowledges, as Ginger did in his somewhat hammy coming down to earth, that he cannot deny his biological imperatives, though he had earlier protested that he no longer needed his family. On one level, this realization implies that the rebellion is over, though not retracted or canceled; on another it is simply a recognition, perhaps more painful for an adolescent hero like Gavin than for Ginger, of the terrible sense of loss inherent in a rebellion against one's family. By creating a new and self-defined relationship with his father, Gavin does not completely dispel this sense, but he does serve notice that the transition from adolescence to adulthood has taken place, and on his terms.

The Emperor of Ice-Cream on the whole fulfills the requirements of the comic mode in fiction, but Moore runs into some of the same kinds of problems here with that approach as he did in *Ginger Coffey*, though that of appropriately distancing himself from his subject is not one of them, as it was in the earlier novel. Rather it is the injection of a number of scenes which in themselves are competently drawn—I am thinking particularly of the Reverend McMurtry scene, or the entire Lambert eviction-reinstatement episode—but which do not mesh easily with the main flow of the novel. Hargreaves's social conscience at best merely serves his selfish indulgence, and for him to leap to Lambert's aid, especially after warning Gavin of his mooching tendencies, on the pretext of helping a victim of the "system," strains our credulity too much. And it is on the whole, too, an awkward way of making it possible for the lapsed Catholic Gavin to discover homosexuality among the Protestants, and the fact that nothing more comes of this meeting except for Gavin's immediate revulsion seems to make the success of such episodes dependent more on their own integral components than on their organic relationship to the novel as a whole. That many of Moore's isolated scenes do have a self-sustaining power attests to his ability to present us with a brilliant sketch, but their effect on the longer work, which demands a sustained comic tone, is not always wholly positive.

As in his earlier Belfast novels, Moore is still concerned in *Emperor* with a relatively insignificant member of society, and again it is his compassion for the "nonheroic hero" that gives this novel its warmth and integrity. In some ways Gavin is as weak as Judith and Dev were, and in a very real sense he had to depend on "luck" even more than Ginger had to. Unlike all those protagonists, however, Gavin operated in a world which was at the point of disintegration, and Moore was more concerned with dramatizing the conjunction of the historical moment with the imaginative protagonist than he was with depicting the nature of social reality. Moore recalled in a letter to an Ulster television producer that one of the things he remembered from his Belfast youth was "the odd, faintly comic set of attitudes with which we in Ulster met the advent of Hitler."[19] *Emperor* allowed him, among other things, to resolve that recollection, while *Judith Hearne* and *Lupercal* evoked the more prosaic social reality of that youth. Taken together, these three Old World novels not only depict graphically the details of an identical setting which paradoxically allows for both defeat and triumph, but reflect an artistry which renders such contradictions convincing.

CHAPTER 4

From the New World

I *Introduction*

ONE of the minor ironies involved in the fictional journey from "Diarmuid Devine, B.A." to "James Francis Coffey, failed B.A." is the supremacy of the failure: Devine's academic achievement traps him forever in the role it has prepared him for, while Ginger's bluffing sustains him, and, indeed, improves his chances, from crisis to crisis. This fact illustrates the nature of the breakthrough that Moore achieved in his third novel, his first of several in which he juxtaposes North American values and experiences against their Irish counterparts. Increasingly from this point on, the voice of the exile is heard in Moore's fiction, whose laments, protestations, and celebrations characteristically come together in a complex pattern that reflects the contradictions and uncertainties, as well as the possibilities, Moore himself experienced in the New World. As a result, these novels on the whole are not as sharply defined or as finite as his two early novels, though they clearly reflect the kind of resolution and tone achieved in his later Belfast novel, *Emperor.*

The emphasis in these novels is on a movement away from themes and issues which have the institutional orientation manifested in *Judith Hearne* and *Lupercal* toward an individual quest for knowledge and moral solutions to problems; identity, rather than conformity or social acceptance, emerges as the overriding concern of their protagonists, even though this pursuit is frequently disturbing and painful. On the surface, Ginger Coffey's problems and his responses to them seem less profound and less significant than either Brendan Tierney's or Fergus Fadden's, but, as will be seen, this has perhaps as much to do with Moore's handling of the comic mode as it has with his conception of Ginger as a human being. All three protagonists have succeeded in doing what neither of the Belfast protagonists could achieve, in that they have made the break from a parochial, deterministic world and have achieved a measure of

sexual fulfillment. On the surface, then, they have divested themselves of the problems which beset Judith and Dev, but, as will be
seen, by this very opting for a pragmatic existence in a less
deterministic world, they take unto themselves problems that their
Belfast counterparts never conceived of. Moore may have moved
away from his concern with the failure to individuals who at the
very least are marginal successes, but their decisions and procrasti-
nations still have a serious moral and ethical significance, and it is
this kind of concern that he exploits in his North American novels.

II   The Luck of Ginger Coffey (1960)[1]

The new ground that Moore breaks in *Ginger Coffey* involves not
only a geographical shift, but an aesthetic and metaphysical shift as
well, for he exploits here the elements of the comic mode to transmit
his altered perception of experience. Essentially, this mode reflects
an interpretation of experience which allows man to accommodate
himself to the inconsistencies and uncertainties of his world, to
triumph even over his own shortcomings, and ultimately to be
reintegrated into the society which at the outset was hostile to his
values and pursuits. Characteristically, it involves a process of self-
discovery in which the self undergoes a transformation from a
stature dictated by some ideal or illusion to one defined by reality,
and this process usually signifies a diminution rather than an
enlargement of self. In short, the comic hero learns to accept his
limitations rather than be defeated by them, and, unlike the tragic
hero, he learns the truth about himself in time to accommodate
himself to his world. "The British comic tradition is one expression
of a confidence that horrors can be handled," the late James Hall
argued in his book *The Tragic Comedians*,[2] and it is this kind of
attitude that is reflected in *Ginger Coffey;* even though Ginger does
not successfully handle all his horrors, he acts as though he can, and
it is this confident bearing toward the world that sets him apart
from Judith and Dev. Dev does achieve, as we have seen, a large
measure of self-knowledge, and in a sense he is the potential comic
hero paralyzed by a society that cannot tolerate that possibility.

At the outset, however, Ginger is close to being, like Judith and
Dev, one of life's losers; indeed, as the new year begins for him, he
is within fifteen dollars and three cents of the bottom. But unlike
them, he exudes nothing but blustering optimism and a resilience
that compel the world at large to share for the moment his own
view of himself as "a Dublin squire." Appropriately, however, it is

on that first working day of the new year that reality overtakes him, and thus he begins his painful decline from crisis to crisis, until, alone in his cell at the very depths of his discontent, he is able to express the obligatory *mea culpa* of the comic hero. To his great wonder, he discovers that this act of confession and acceptance of his reduced state creates another dimension of experience of which he was previously unaware, and that it removes his fears of what would transpire once his ideal self had disintegrated. In a very real sense he achieves "the ultimate in comic sublimity," which, as Cyrus Hoy explains, "is evident when the worst, which has long been taking shape in the affairs of men, is not realized. In such a case, the protagonist of comedy finds himself saved, as it were, in despite of himself."[3]

Being saved "in despite of himself" is essentially the story of Ginger's life, but it is not only "luck," as the ironic title suggests, that works for him, for he has an incurably honest approach to the *ethics* of his situation if not to the *facts*. Albert Camus has said that "a man defines himself by his make-believe as well as by his sincere impulses,"[4] and for most of the novel it is the make-believe elements in Ginger's life that he consistently lives by. It is important to note, however, that this framework is not an end in itself, and it does not serve solely as a mechanism for evading responsibility; on the contrary, it is the means by which he pursues his most important concern, the preservation of his love for his family. This is the larger truth he is concerned with, the overriding truth which he valiantly tries to create by some alchemy of telling lies—to Veronica about the return tickets and his salary, to the employment clerk about his credentials, to MacGregor about his newspaper experience, and so on. Marvelously, all these lies work, in that they do sustain him from crisis to crisis, with the result that he does preserve his family; as Hoy points out, it is to such an end that the actions of the comic hero converge:

Comedy ends with the restoration of the individual to himself, and to all that, in the widest sense, can be said to give him his identity. He will have lost it . . . through sundry transgressions, follies, and inconsistencies; also through the force of the sundry delusions which he has entertained, and which keep him from knowing himself or his proper good. But his proper good is defined for him at last, he has the wit to see it for what it is, and it is still—wonderful to relate—within his grasp, which is not the least of the marvels which comedy celebrates.[5]

Throughout the novel it was the exalted views he held of himself, whether the Old World "Dublin squire" or the New World "Coffey of the *Tribune*," that prevented him from recognizing "his proper good," and his struggles to overcome this problem are both comic and pathetic. What was essentially involved was the progressive stripping away of his assumed cloaks of identity, a process which takes Ginger through a number of personal crises, betrayals, and other nightmarish experiences in which he is exposed to facets of reality he had never before encountered. In a literal sense these episodes—his stint as a galley slave, his diaper delivery job, his assignation with the call-girl, his arrest and trial—spell out shock, guilt, and mortification for Ginger, but on another level they constitute an obligatory ritual through which he moves from near oblivion to self-recognition, realizable only when he was prepared "to abandon the facts of his life for the facts of the world" (*GC*, 118).

In all these episodes, Moore is careful to emphasize the essential isolation of Coffey; like his fellow exiles, Brendan Tierney and Fergus Fadden, Ginger discovers that severing the bonds of the Old World produces loneliness in the New, for here there is no institutional or social framework to comfort one. Thus, when Ginger descends to his proofreader's job at the *Tribune*, he is cut off from his family, evicted from his quarters, and compelled to part from the landlady's son, Michel, the only consistent admirer he has had in Canada. This parting is, however, attended by a significant gesture: he gives Michel the Alpine buttons and brush from his hat, an act which constitutes Ginger's first step in divesting himself of the external manifestations of his assumed poses; it indicates, too, that he is moving away from the world of make-believe and toys that had held him and Michel together and had seriously blinded Ginger to the nature of adult reality.

His temporary sojourn in a cell-like room in the YMCA marks the extremity of this stage of Ginger's isolation, a situation which produces for him the epiphanylike awareness that "for the first time in fifteen years no one in the world knew where Ginger Coffey was. For the first time in fifteen years, he had stopped running" (*GC*, 103-104). This somewhat exciting realization tempts him momentarily to assume the ultimate state of exile, "to retire from the struggle, live like a hermit, unknown and unloved in this faraway land" (*GC*, 104), but it is not long before the assumption and obligations of a normal sexual and family relationship override this solipsistic impulse. Coffey soon receives "ocular proof" that his rationalizations were the correct ones, in the person of the eccentric W. K. Wilson, "no longer a boy," but who still lived in "a world of toys." Wilson argues correctly that Coffey's problem "is a problem in human relationships" and his human solution to it contributes very clearly to Ginger's goal of preserving his family. But nevertheless he is not a person whom Ginger wishes to emulate, even though he was "a man who could still dream youth's dreams . . . , living life's adventures . . . , an old dream of Coffey's" (*GC*, 111). For, like old Billy Davis later on, Wilson stands as a warning to Ginger:

> The thin neck was clawed with age; there were gray streaks in the long untidy locks of hair; the hands were veiny, stippled with telltale brown moles. Was manhood what Wilson had missed? (*GC*, 111)

His own manhood held in suspension for the moment, Ginger accepts Wilson's former job, and this decision compels him to complete the already-begun process of stripping off the last vestiges of his Dublin-squire persona: "Off went his Tyrolean hat, his hacking jacket, his gray tweed trousers and brown suède boots. On the bench they lay, the last remains of Ginger Coffey. On went the uniform, anonymous and humiliating," but which, significantly, "fitted him perfectly" (*GC*, 114, 115). His anonymity is for the moment essential, a necessary stage between the discarding of his false persona and the assumption of his true one, but the fact that he is soon recognized by some former Dublin residents indicates that he cannot remain anonymous for long. This recognition scene is a crucial one for Coffey: past reputation and present reality come together with an epiphanic significance as he discards forever the hold that the past has had over him: "What did it matter? What did they matter, so long as he was not going home? And in that moment he knew that, sink or swim, Canada was home now, for better or for worse, for richer or for poorer, until death" (*GC*, 133).

Coffey's articulation of this credo in the language of the marriage ceremony underscores the relationship that exists between his two main concerns, preserving his family and justifying his exile to Canada in the first place. The two are obviously related in strictly realistic terms, as the domestic quarrels within the Coffey family clearly illustrate. But the commitment to exile was far more than an economic or social one for Coffey, for it really represented an existential protest against a closed world, and an intuitive belief that one can only find his true identity through pragmatic, rather than prescribed, pursuits and experiences. Thus Ginger's rather rhapsodic opting for Canadian exile marks a real turning point in his quest for self-knowledge and identity; he has at this point, though he does not as yet consciously know it, accommodated himself to his absurd world where he can handle most of its "horrors." One evidence of this is that he backs out of the prearranged adultery scene with Melody Ward which would have given Veronica her divorce, though he stands by his promise to release her when his anticipated promotion fails to materialize. Though he would lose his wife in either situation, to do so under the first circumstance would be to reestablish his anonymity and insignificance; under the second circumstance, his integrity and unselfishness.

This moral reaffirmation sustains him during his arrest and trial, and it is in his lowest descent into the equivalent of Conrad's "destructive element" that he finally achieves a full recognition of his nature and of his responsiblity for his dilemma:

He stepped back, trying to peer sideways down the corridor and, as he did, he saw his own face, angled in the reflection from the glass pane. He stared at that sad impostor, at that hateful, stupid man. . . . He knew something now, something he had not known before. A man's life was nobody's fault but his own. Not God's, not Vera's, not even Canada's. His own fault. *Mea culpa*. (*GC*, 222-23)

The court's subsequent leniency toward Ginger stands within this perspective as a symbolic gesture in recognition of the new man Ginger has become, and the fulfillment he experiences on the courthouse steps suggests that he has transcended forever his previous self-imposed limitations.

Ginger's reconciliation with Veronica constitutes a logical consequence of this rebirth and of his recognition by Canada as a person deserving of a second chance. Like Gabriel Conroy of Joyce's "The Dead," Ginger has come to recognize the difference between self-delusion and *mea culpa*, between lust and love, between dreams and reality, and he thus establishes some basic criteria on which to proceed in a world that he is just beginning to understand. It is these intuitive feelings and impulses that spell the difference between fulfillment and despair for the comic hero, especially in a world where traditional social and religious responses have lost their usefulness.

But if Ginger recalls Gabriel Conroy in this final view of experience, the more pertinent Joycean comparison throughout his fluctuating odyssey is with Leopold Bloom. It is the discrepancy between the intention and the reality which Camus sees as the basis of the absurd, and both Bloom and Coffey define themselves almost exclusively in terms of intention. In this respect, James Hall's comment on Bloom—"everything stops him in real life, but nothing stops his games"[6]—applies with equal relevance to Coffey, for they both display a remarkable disregard for the realities of their dilemmas, though both compensate for this liability by consistently standing for human dignity. Thus Ginger's reneging on the adultery plan is simply his reassertion of the more fundamental and dignified relationship with his family, and his rejection of the call-girl has its Joycean parallel in Bloom's rejection of meretricious enchantments of Bella Cohen's brothel. And at the end of their odyssey, the new relationship that Coffey and Bloom establish with their wives reflects their coming-of-age and their acceptance of a new reality about themselves.

In *Ginger Coffey*, Moore's departure from the prevailing realism of his first two novels in favor of a more impressionistic and flexible style produces mixed results, and it is significant that only in *The Emperor of Ice-Cream* did Moore again resort to the comic mode. His wish to move beyond realism was inevitable, given the kind of finite perfection he achieved in his Belfast novels, and Montreal posed for him a far more complex setting than did Belfast, and one that in a sense defied a literal and logical description. Possibly because he did not understand Montreal as intimately as he did Belfast, his earlier obsession with the stultifying effects of environment on character gives way here to a consideration of the *carpe diem* philosophy which he saw as a manifestation of a New World outlook. In this world, the moments of potential failure from which one can redeem oneself are more numerous than they were in Belfast, and thus the failure to seize one particular moment does not produce the lifetime of irrevocable failure it did for Judith and Devine. "[Ginger's] fault," Moore observed, "is that he doesn't see the moment when it comes. He will always bypass his chance and go on to something else."[7] The novel's resolution suggests that he will probably go back to the diaper position, but in a pinch he can always follow Wilson to Blind River; the very fact that there is "something else" to turn to will undoubtedly continue to sustain Ginger, though he will undoubtedly go through life close to being

one of life's losers. It is interesting, too, in light of Jamie Mangan's
reporter experiences that he recalls in *The Mangan Inheritance,* to
speculate on what Ginger might have been in for had he in fact
realized his dream of becoming a *Tribune* reporter: "a round of
endless, dull local stories, at the beck of . . . a doltish management
lackey who turned out an uninspired set of local pages . . ." (*MI,*
63).

Moore's impressionistic portrait of Montreal constitutes one of the
strengths of this novel, and it lends to Ginger's odyssey a somewhat
surrealistic effect, particularly in the proofreading episodes and in
the courtroom scene. Ginger's descent from his initial goal of
"Executive and Professional" to the reality of proofreader is swift
and inexorable, and on the way he is confronted by a succession of
individuals who together constitute the entrenchment of class and
privilege in Montreal: Donnelly, Beauchemin, Kahn, Grosvenor,
MacGregor. This kind of social determinism, based on favoritism,
influence, or patronage, operates with as much effect as did its
counterpart in Dublin, and, as a new Canadian, Ginger had not only
to manipulate "the facts of his life," but to overcome the establishment's suspicion and hostility just barely disguised beneath the
veneer of time-worn labels and clichés about the Irish. It is the last
of these individuals, appropriately labeled by Ginger as a "sulphur-
breathing Scottish Beelzebub" who relegates him to the lowly
proofreader's position, where he becomes part of a bizarre group of
misfits: a cripple, a stammerer, a homosexual, and an aged, sick
Irish immigrant who poses a disturbing omen for Ginger. In a
drunken and grotesque initiatory ceremony in the local tavern, they
try to identify Ginger's problem, and in a parody of the exile's
dream Fox gives his vision of Canada as seen from the bottom:

"I have to explain the facts of life to our immigrant brother. . . . The
twentieth century belongs to Canada. And if it does, then you had better
know our values. Remember that in this fair city of Montreal the owner of
a department store is a more important citizen than any judge of the
Superior Court. Never forget that, Paddy boy. Money is the root of all good
here. One nation, indivisible, under Mammon that's our heritage." (*GC,*
70)

It is in the courtroom scene, where Ginger is being tried on the
charge of "*a fait pisser juste dans la grande porte du Royal Family
Hotel*" (*GC,* 221), where this view of Canada is in a sense put to the

test. This episode takes on a Kafkaesque dimension, with justice being dispensed within the framework of some absurd nightmare, but the prevailing atmosphere in the courtroom toward Ginger is clearly one of sympathy and amusement rather than hostility. In succinct phrases and set scenes, Moore captures the essence of Montreal's social conflicts, between French and English, between police and their victims, between police and the judiciary, and in his humane sentencing of Ginger the judge gives the lie to Fox's earlier disparaging assessment of his influence: "I am dealing with you leniently, Coffey, because I am sorry for your family. To be alone in a new country, with their breadwinner in jail, seems to me a fate which your wife and child do not deserve" (*GC*, 233).

Between the world of the proofreaders and the courtroom lies a world, represented by Wilson and Brott, which demands in effect only a kind of unlimited pragmatism and compromise deriving from one's needs and capabilities. It is in such a world, free of the entrenched values of the class system, whether of Dublin or of Montreal, that the Ginger Coffeys will find some measure of fulfillment and recognition. If the world has no finite values, then, as Camus observed, the quantity of experiences becomes as important as the quality of experience, and from this perspective Coffey's service as "a member of the shit brigade" becomes as significant as "Coffey of the *Tribune*," a realization that he finally comes to himself. In retrospect, though Ginger seems to be thrown from disaster to disaster, the only human betrayals he experiences in the New World are those perpetrated by Grosvenor and MacGregor. Ironically it is their betrayals he capitalizes on to effect the reunion with his family, and his assumption at his trial of the name Gerald MacGregor indicts his only real enemies in Montreal more than it does himself.

There are many standard requirements of the comic mode that are successfully met by *Ginger Coffey*, such as the instinct for self-preservation, the restoration of the hero, the defeat of the impostor figure (in this case not only Grosvenor, but that aspect of Coffey himself that he sees as "that sad impostor"), and the completion of the mythic cycle that was implied by the beginning. Yet general opinion holds that *Ginger Coffey* is not an entirely successful work, that it lacks the emotional impact of Moore's first two novels and the formal sophistication of such later ones as *Mary Dunne* and *The Great Victorian Collection*. On the first point, perhaps it is a matter of the comic hero not eliciting the same kind of response as a tragic hero, because the latter is pitted against obstacles which seem more cosmic and ominous than those faced by the comic hero. But even so, Ginger lacks a very important dimension that Moore successfully developed not only with Judith and Devine, but also with his other comic hero, Gavin Burke, and that is a convincing introspective nature. This deficiency in Ginger's character undoubtedly reflects the question of Moore's aesthetic distance, for he was more detached from his Belfast protagonists than he was from Coffey, and in those scenes demanding detachment Moore does not appear to suspend sufficiently his own affiliations with Ginger's experiences.

Structurally, too, *Ginger Coffey* reflects some weaknesses uncharacteristic of his novels in general. In particular, the Veronica-Grosvenor affair fails to elicit the criterion of inevitability that obtains, for example, with Jane and Vito in *Limbo* or with Sheila and Tom in *The Doctor's Wife*. Grosvenor's designs upon Veronica had grown in proportion to Ginger's failures, but we do not learn enough about either Gerry or Veronica to justify their liaison aesthetically. Veronica's attraction to him is not sexual, as is the case with Jane and Sheila, and Ginger's amazement that she should be attracted to this "self-important dummy" is, I think, shared by the reader: in his manly capacities as lover, fighter, or drinker, Grosvenor is clearly inferior to Ginger. He illustrates, it is true, the proofreaders' views of who is important in Canadian life, but ultimately he must be seen as one of the near-caricatures Moore has drawn from his Canadian experiences, and who is to emerge again more devastatingly as R. M. MacKinnon, the "Warm Brown Turd" in *Mary Dunne*.

Stylistically, *Ginger Coffey* anticipates both *Limbo* and *Fergus* in its experimentation, and to a certain extent *The Mangan Inheritance* in its mixture of modes. "I tried to mix three styles in this novel:" Moore has stated, "realistic style, comedy, and tragedy, and to do something that actually could happen realistically in certain scenes in the book in a farcical way. To lift it out of flat realism."[8] Though he achieves some brilliant effects in this way—notably the YMCA scene, the tavern scenes, and the courtroom scene—there is occasionally a straining for comic effect, and at times a confusion as to whether a scene is meant to be farcical or serious. Moore displays consistently, however, a discerning eye for vivid detail, a keen ear for the polyglot of cosmopolitan Montreal, and an experiential familiarity with the life and vigor of a wintry city.

In terms of vision, setting, and technique *Ginger Coffey* represents an important development in Moore's fiction. On a personal level, it marks the beginning of the exile's attempt to accommodate himself to a bewildering world and to exorcise his Old World roots, an attempt that continues in *Limbo* and will in one sense be completed in *Fergus*. But in another sense, this process becomes more difficult from book to book, for Ginger has only himself and his memories to contend with, while Brendan and Fergus have visitations from both the living and the dead.

III   An Answer from Limbo *(1962)*[9]

In his fourth novel, Moore continues the odyssey of the exile figure in North America, but this time with a protagonist and an environment far more complex than those he revealed in *Ginger Coffey*. In a sense, Brendan Tierney begins where Ginger left off, having attained a tolerable foothold and security in the New World and sharing a family relationship which quite clearly is a compromise rather than an ideal. Ginger is prepared to accept this; Brendan, ten years younger and a talented writer, is not, and it is his resulting domestic, moral, and aesthetic dilemmas that shape the richness and complexity of this novel.

Moore has made a number of statements about the genesis and nature of *An Answer from Limbo* in which he has set forth basically a three-fold purpose. "I wanted to put Irish Catholicism against the rootless wasteland of North America," he said in a radio interview in Canada,[10] and the juxtaposition of these essentially irreconcilable viewpoints gives the novel much of its dramatic tension. On another occasion he said that "it is a book about ambition. I lived in Greenwich Village for two years and became enormously aware of the tremendous amount of ambition—self-defeating ambition— which I saw among people. . . . So what I was trying to show in *An Answer from Limbo* was the effect of ambition on one of its characters."[11] The third concern, the problem of the artist, particularly the exiled artist, in relation to his world is clearly related to the larger theme of identity which increasingly became part of Moore's work starting with *Ginger Coffey*. "I think there has always been this dichotomy in a real writer," Moore explained. "He wants to be terribly human, and he responds emotionally, and at the same time there's this cold observer who cannot cry."[12] In his working notes for *Limbo*, Moore commented further on this dilemma, giving expression, too, to his own artistic credo:

American writing today reflects American society: its absence of ideals, its concern with the private self [which] . . . has narrowed to the point of narcissism: we no longer understand even the smallest widening of the ripples around the pool in which our faces are reflected. . . . There are people who would say today that Brendan . . . is completely justified in ditching his mother, his wife and his children for the sake of his art. But the art he attempts to practice is the novel: a novelist is a moralist and his sense of morality should carry over into his own life, otherwise he is a false prophet preaching a message he does not believe in. It seems to me that private ambition, which has been exalted in our society, is ultimately self-destructive.[13]

By examining the nature of the various conflicts largely within one family, Moore both creates a workable structural framework and achieves a humanization of what might otherwise remain intellectual abstractions. That the family in question is divided against itself in doctrinal and moral issues allows for both symbolic and realistic development of characters, and Brendan, Jane, and Mrs. Tierney very readily assume these dimensions. In broad terms, those portions of the novel given over to Brendan trace the effect of ambition on the writer, those devoted to Jane, the rootlessness and sordidness of materialistic America, and those devoted to Brendan's mother, the opposition between a past governed by spiritual values and a present shaped by materialism and secular chaos. Just as the three individuals in question, however, are very much affected by each other's actions, so these three themes are inextricably linked, and not nearly so distinct as my schematization suggests.

In his manipulations of these dramatized perspectives, Moore is far more experimental with form and point of view than he was in his earlier works, though some of these aesthetic tendencies were apparent in *Judith Hearne* and *Ginger Coffey*. But in *Limbo* they are both more sophisticated and more productive: Brendan's first-person sections ensure his centrality in the novel, but the modified and somewhat subjective third-person sections given over to Jane and Mrs. Tierney serve to emphasize the precariousness of his position. The oblique shots of Brendan, too, presented through a number of peripheral characters, particularly Ted Ormsby in Belfast and Max Bronstein in New York, remind us of the inextricability of his artistic ambitions and his moral expediency, a nexus that is compounded of what seems to be about equal proportions of talent, insecurity, guilt, and a desire for revenge.

In an earlier overture to this novel, "Preliminary Pages for a Work of Revenge," Moore had presented a disturbing foreshadowing of how this artist-sufferer figure might conduct himself, but *Limbo* is more than a mere fleshing out of that sketch. In depicting Brendan's progress from the Belfast setting of Ormsby's question about whom he is prepared to sacrifice for his art to his experiential discovery of *an* answer from the limbo of the New World, Moore so counterbalances point of view in this novel and manipulates its formal and structural components as to underscore the existential nature of this quest. Both the title and the unfolding of the novel indicate that there is in Moore's expanding vision no such thing as *the* answer to a question of this complexity, and the reader is ultimately left to make the final moral and aesthetic judgment on Brendan's conclusion.

In the first three sections of the novel—that is, before Mrs. Tierney arrives in New York—we become aware of the basically incompatible dispositions of the three protagonists: Brendan's ambition, selfishness, and ruthlessness, Jane's emptiness, frustrations, and latent nymphomania, and Mrs. Tierney's sense of order, her prejudice, and her complex feelings of guilt. Brendan's problem initially is how to resolve the conflict between his ambition and his domestic responsibilities; his solution—to bring his mother from Belfast to look after the children while Jane works—is characteristically selfish and simplistic. Throughout the novel he is to be frequently reminded, by Jane, by Pat Gallery, by his mother, of his propensity and readiness to sacrifice others, but his obsession with his book blinds him to the ramifications of his behavior. As with the nameless narrator of "Preliminary Pages," Brendan was goaded into his literary ambition by the taunts of the world, and his getting even with that world is not the least of his motivations, though, undisputedly, his proven talent also justifies his attempt to find a solution.

Jane's problem is fundamentally more serious and more pervasive than Brendan's, for it is not of the kind that can be solved financially or economically. Hers is a spiritual malaise and an emptiness that can only temporarily be fulfilled by giving in to her erotic fantasies; in a very real sense she is an ordinary person trying to find satisfaction in a world whose values and demands seem antithetical to that pursuit. In her own actions and words, Jane both personifies and perpetuates the spiritual and moral bankruptcy of her society, though by novel's end she has achieved a large measure of self-knowledge and dignity. At the outset, however, she is presented almost as a stereotype of the emancipated woman who, in the words of Granville Hicks, "looks on religion as a vulgar superstition, but uses the jargon of psychoanalysis as if it were revealed truth."[14] In her search for significance and meaning as an individual, and in her belief that this quest is in large part tied to sexual fulfillment, she anticipates both Mary Dunne and Sheila Redden; in her inability to distinguish initially between the sexual act as a creative experience and as a fantasy fulfillment, however, she is more like Judith Hearne and ends up, like her, both wiser and sadder.

It is into this world of ambition and emptiness that Brendan brings his mother, and his first view of her after seven years brings home to him the irony of his earlier simple solution, for he realizes the gap between them can never be bridged. Steeped in the traditions of the Old World and in the doctrines of Roman Catholicism, Mrs. Tierney is ignorant and prejudiced. Her anti-Semitic remarks immediately establish a hostility between herself and Jane and her ignorance of the nature of Brendan's talent makes it impossible for her to make any compromises. Yet on the whole it is Mrs. Tierney who monopolizes the reader's sympathy, for by subscribing to some values she is the only one of the three who transcends an exclusive consideration with self, and meets most of her crises with a strong measure of dignity. Ironically, however, by novel's end she and Jane have in a sense reversed their positions, having met each other at the halfway point in a kind of guilty but mutual acceptance of infidelities and sexual fantasies; Jane's impulsive gesture of love toward her near the end reflects her new stature, and is rendered all the more poignant by Mrs. Tierney's refusal to accept it.

In the novel, Moore has many occasions to reveal the relationship between his artistry and his grasp, as an exile, of the cultural shock which Mrs. Tierney experienced in the New World. Particularly effective is the episode of her arrival in New York—the airport scene, the taxi ride, her meeting with Jane and the grandchildren—scenes in which Moore combines the realism of physical details with subjective, almost surrealistic, impressions of these details to emphasize the prevailing polarity which will run through the novel. At the airport itself are presented two impressions of what the New World represents to Brendan and his mother, and the difference in their reactions is not merely a question of familiarity versus unfamiliarity. Brendan's embracing of this world is described in terms of its mechanical efficiency:

But this morning, as I got off the bus at the airport, as I went through a door which opened by electric eye, and rode up on a moving staircase to the observation lounge, I knew that it is this world I care about, this world of moving staircases, electric eyes, efficient loudspeakers. Exile now means exile from this. My island is no longer home. (*AL*, 30)

His mother's fear of this world derives from the sudden expansion of her human horizons, and she desperately clings to the comfort of what is familiar to her: "She was glad of Brendan: this place was foreign from the first go-off, what with niggers in red caps asking for your bags. She had never before in her life spoken to a black man" (*AL*, 32). Throughout the novel, it is Mrs. Tierney's human relationships which sustain her, particularly those which involve other isolated and lonely individuals, like her cousin and the woman she meets in the park, whereas Brendan is always depicted in a fractured or abrasive relationship with human beings. It is not the least of the ironies of this novel that his exaltation of the mechanical conveniences of the New World appropriately reaps its reward near the end of the novel as, at his mother's funeral, he watches her "mechanized last descent" into her grave (*AL*, 321).

In another crucial scene, the taxi ride from the airport, Moore effectively establishes the Catholic-wasteland dichotomy that characterizes much of the novel. This trip through the surrealistic cityscape of New York, with its "vistas of glass, poured concrete and steel . . . [and] intestines of huge, multicolored machines" (*AL*, 33), becomes for Mrs. Tierney a metaphorical journey into darkness, for just as the taxi enters the Midtown tunnel, she learns that her grandchildren have not been baptized, and momentary dizziness and blackness overcome her. A confused chanting chorus develops in her mind, as her misgivings are alternated with the roar of traffic and scenes of unreality:

Pagans. Not baptized.
Everything was so high, so tall . . . . this huddle of great upended cartons, a man was like a fly beside them—
My grandchildren are heathens.
Dirt. Gray grime over so much of it, wastes of paper blowing about in the gutters. . . .
Not baptized.
Glimpsed for a moment, an old boozer lying in a doorway. . . . (*AL*, 37)

Limbo of course is the place where, among other things, unbaptized children are confined, and Mrs. Tierney's subsequent resolution to redress this situation serves only to intensify her own isolation from the family; ironically, far from rescuing anybody from the limbo they all inhabit, it becomes the precipitating act toward her own eviction and ultimate death.

Both literally and symbolically, the baptismal ceremony that Mrs. Tierney performs constitutes the ultimate and irreconcilable issue which separates these two worlds; as an expression of belief in traditional values, it serves as well to elevate Mrs. Tierney above the inhabitants of Brendan's world. Yet Moore ironically juxtaposes the two kinds of worlds within the Tierney household to suggest there is something irrelevant in both. On the one hand, he sets up the baptismal scene in the bathroom, with a plastic mouthrinse cup as the holy vessel, and the children asking irreverent questions like "Who's the father? Daddy? And who's the ghost?" and "What good is this game?" And Mrs. Tierney all the while watches herself guiltily in the mirror. On the other hand, a second ritual of mumbo-jumbo is simultaneously in progress in the living room, where various individuals are holding forth in Freudian and psychoanalytic jargon, trading opinions about "phallic females" achieving "cultural dominance on the mass level," and about the reduction of "every female aspiration to simple penis envy" (*AL*, 133). The level of conversation here may be more sophisticated than that going on in the bathroom, but Moore seems to suggest that the efficacy of both rituals is about the same.

These ceremonies serve in addition to emphasize the increasing isolation of both Mrs. Tierney and Jane, who from this point on are perhaps more in league with each other than either one would care to admit. The elements of mutual guilt obviously operate here—on Mrs. Tierney because of her interference with the children, and on Jane because of her barely controlled lust for Vito—but neither feels morally or psychologically at ease with Brendan's friends, "these drunken shouters of balls and filth, these lunatics who believed in nothing but their own mad selves" (*AL*, 139). Jane in fact had to remind Brendan that she was home, and she soon withdrew and "sat on the windowseat, looking tired and out of things" (*AL*, 139), a foreshadowing of the existential isolation she experiences near the end of the novel on her return to New York from Saratoga. Mrs. Tierney, also "unnoticed . . . got up and left the room, . . . went down the hall and entered her little cell" (*AL*, 139), where the next day she exchanges the "heathen Chinee" print for a crucifix; in addition to its restoration of her accustomed world and values, this act significantly makes manifest her new relationship with Jane, on whose back the previous evening she had noticed "a thin crucifix of perspiration" as she bent to kiss the children, and "suddenly she felt a quick sympathy" (*AL*, 137) for Jane. Not the least poignant aspect of this novel is that these two isolated women, equally the victims of Brendan's obsessions and selfishness, never can articulate to each other this inchoate love and understanding.

Nevertheless, in both their literal and symbolic manifestations, Mrs. Tierney's two religious performances have disturbing consequences. Jane's irrational outburst reflects all her pent-up frustrations and her basic inability to counter Mrs. Tierney's statements with a matching dignity, and in a sense represents an obligatory response to her earlier concern that "nothing ever seemed to turn out just as it should, not her looks, not her sex life, not even her kids: nothing ever had and perhaps nothing ever would" (*AL*, 125). By reestablishing her authority in her own house where Brendan— St. Brendan the Hypocrite, he calls himself—characteristically refuses to side openly with either her or his mother, she begins the process of defining herself in terms of the pragmatic necessities of her world. The human price, however, is high, and Mrs. Tierney, dejected and unwanted, begins her brief and fatal sojourn at her cousin's flat.

Before she is evicted, however, the ramifications of her two acts are symbolically visited upon her during a disturbing nightmare. In a scene reminiscent of Leopold Bloom's mock trial in the brothel scene in *Ulysses,* and one which anticipates the kangaroo court scenes of *Fergus,* her past actions are brought to judgment before the various figures in her life; where she thought she was performing good works, a succession of witnesses see only vanity, selfishness, and deceit. Fundamentally, however, their accusations echo her own doubts and fears about her actions, and perhaps even about the whole doctrine of the Church. At one point in this surrealistic trial, the judge, who is actually her father, asks her to look for Lisa and Liam in Limbo (ironically a place like an airport lounge), and when she could not find them, he levels at her the most devastating charge of all: "You baptized them. You denied them even the consolation of this place of neglect. You made them Christians, but you did not prepare them as Christians" (*AL*, 212-13).

The measure of any values subscribed to in this life, however, cannot really be known until one is at the point of leaving it, and within this perspective Moore's ultimate statement on the power of faith is a positive one. As Mrs. Tierney lies neglected and dying on

the floor of Frank Finnerty's apartment, she experiences a vision
similar to her earlier nightmare, but this time its components spell
out ecstasy rather than despair:

"Come," said her father. And he took her hands and joined them with the
hands of her grandchildren, and her grandchildren led her across the room
into heaven as everyone clapped and clapped and clapped— (AL, 274-75)

This fantasy of a chorus in heaven is juxtaposed against the reality
of incessant noise from the television set, a convincingly appropriate
symbol of the impersonal and unfeeling world with which she had
vainly tried to come to terms. One of her earlier misgivings about
America centered on the fact "that she had never seen a funeral
passing in the streets" (AL, 69), and a major aesthetic strength of
the way Moore depicts her own death resides in the way it is
juxtaposed against a backdrop of this very indifference. "Fancy me
lying here," she muses, "and the people on the telly looking at me,
talking away, smiling at me, the telly is like the world, people
looking at you but not seeing you" (AL, 290). Ironically, too, the
offerings of the television set—a weather forecast, a queen-for-a-day
pageant, a headache commercial—are only slightly more irrelevant
than Brendan's actions out in the real world. "She lay dying on the
floor of a strange apartment," he guiltily acknowledges later, "while
I, her son, ran senseless about the city, quibbling over words" (AL,
314).

    In contrast to Brendan's obsessive search for the elusive, Mrs.
Tierney's quiet but determined plea for a simple sense of order is a
powerful and moving justification of her way of looking at the
world:

I want: my own room in my own house, my own brass bed, my own good
sheets, a nice nightie on me and my hair done. I want the house tidy and
drink and food downstairs for the people coming in. I want a priest, I want
the last sacraments, I want Mass cards and a funeral at home and my place
beside Grattan on the hill. I want to die in my own place, not here. Not
here. (AL, 289)

Mrs. Tierney's values clearly sustain her dignity in facing both life
and death, and this is one measure of her moral superiority over
Brendan and Jane. In weighing Irish Roman Catholicism against
American restlessness as a viable set of values, Moore is frequently
critical of both in respect of some of their manifestations; yet the

implications of this novel clearly spell out that even a wrong faith can mold a stronger character than no faith at all.

Mrs. Tierney's earlier question about whether it was America's fault or hers for the way Brendan turned out bears directly on other themes of this novel, particularly the effect of ambition upon a writer, and the problem of identity for the artist in exile. The novel itself appropriately dramatizes rather than simplifies these questions, and much of the hold that Brendan has on the reader derives from his own genuine confusion about who he is and what he is doing. Outside of the novel, however, Moore has made some comments which are relevant to Brendan's situation:

> I lived in Greenwich Village at the time of writing [*Limbo*], and I noticed that the serious writers there . . . were quite interested in best sellerdom, publicity, immediate personal fame. . . . I think the temptations for the serious American writer today are fame and fortune. Nobody understands the old idea—that there should be a company of the good, and the fact that your books don't sell a hundred thousand copies . . . isn't the real answer. Brendan was caught between the two: He really wanted to be a great success, and he wanted to be a good writer.[15]

When the novel opens, Brendan is suspended between the aspirations fostered by his childhood agonies and determinations and the present reality of his tangible achievements—six published short stories and an unfinished novel. His belief that he has genuine talent is shared by his literary acquaintances and by publishers who have read his works, and his obsession to prove this to the world is fed by the successes of those he considers his inferiors. "How many works of the imagination have been goaded into life," he muses, "by envy of an untalented contemporary's success" (*AL*, 10), and throughout *Limbo*, the specter of the published Max Bronstein continues to haunt and disturb him. From time to time, but particularly after he has resigned his job to devote full time to his novel, he experiences reservations about his talent and about the sacrifices he is demanding of others:

> But O God, O God, will I succeed? Will I be able to revenge myself on the past by transforming it into a world of words? . . . If I am wrong, if I am setting out to do something I am not fit to do, then am I not assuming the most despicable of roles? For who is more contemptible than the false artist, posturing through life as he spews out his tiny frauds? What spectacle more degrading than the lives of these Village Rimbauds, covered in the vomit of

sickly pastiche, crying out their genius and their purity from mouths filled
with rotten teeth? Am I now to be one of them? (*AL*, 60)

There is enough evidence in *Limbo* to confirm that Brendan is
sufficiently talented and conscientious to render these rhetorical
questions more dramatic than relevant in this case; they do point,
however, to the literary types that inhabit his world, who are well
represented, for example, at Dortmunder's party, with its "promising young writer of forty," "an unpublished playwright," and
Dortmunder himself, "a marginal producer of documentary films"
(*AL*, 71). Though we never do learn very much about the nature of
Brendan's novel, it is clear that it will become both a critical and a
popular success, and his obsessed protestations to Gerston about
proposed cuts and changes seem to derive more from vanity than
from artistic considerations.

Give and take a few delays, then, Brendan does in fact live up to
his end of the domestic arrangement reluctantly agreed to by his
wife and his mother, and in effect achieves his lifelong ambition to
become a novelist. In the process, of course, he has provided an
affirmative answer to Ted Ormsby's long-standing question about
whether he would be prepared to sacrifice himself for his art. With
the publication of his first story some several years earlier, he had
exulted over the fact that he had freed himself of his parents' world
forever, and now, ironically, this has irrevocably come true. For his
novel, which he had in its early stages called his "loved but ailing
child," comes into full life, as it were, at the precise moment he
receives news of his mother's death. At the Dortmunder party,
Brendan had made a prophetic statement which established the
posture that a dedicated writer has to assume, a definition which at
this crucial juncture applies to him with precise relevance: "Standing by his wife's bedside watching her face contort, the better to
record her death agony. Taking mental notes so that he can write
about it later. . . . Because he can't help doing it. He's not human:
he's a writer. He can't feel: he can only record" (*AL*, 72).

In this way Moore links the themes of the problem of the artist
and the question of identity, for by assuming this stance, Brendan
in effect relinquishes or subordinates those aspects of his identity
normally made manifest in his other roles—son, husband, father,
friend—and he has progressively become unrecognizable in these
relationships. "What kin was that boy to this stranger?" Mrs.
Tierney wonders shortly after her arrival (*AL*, 35), and by novel's

end Jane sees him as "a person strange and familiar to her as her parents had been strange yet familiar when she was a little girl: a figure without whose protection and help life would be uncertain and difficult. And that is all, she said" (*AL*, 308); in other words, no longer a husband in the full sense of the word. Throughout his odyssey, Brendan is dimly aware of his altering relationships with the people in his world, but it is not until his mother's death that he understands fully the nature of his metamorphosis:

O Mamma, I sacrificed you; I see your yellow face. Jane, I abandoned you: I look at you now and know that all is changed. Am I still my mother's son, my wife's husband, the father of my children? Or am I a stranger, strange even to myself? (*AL*, 319)

And as his mother's funeral concludes, he recalls his prophetic words, and seeing himself, as it were, for the first time from the outside, as that "curiously vulgar watcher," he knows finally the answer to Ormsby's question: "I have altered beyond all self-recognition. I have lost and sacrificed myself" (*AL*, 322).

Brendan's journey to self-knowledge is far and away the most destructive—both to self and to others—of the many such quests that characterize Moore's fiction; in comparison, for example, Dev's and Ginger's dilemmas constitute little more than the occasional mirror-gazing and a final readiness to say *mea culpa*. Indeed, alone of Moore's characters, Brendan never does take the blame to the point where he will act for the good of others; though his selfish neglect clearly led to his mother's death, he protested angrily to Jane that "it's nobody's fault," and "remembered that [he] had not wept, would not weep, for what [he] felt was guilt, not sorrow; shock, not loss" (*AL*, 318). In much the same way he had earlier feared whether he could become a successful writer, he now ponders the ultimate value of what he has accomplished, and, as before, this dilemma too is posited through a series of rhetorical questions:

Will my writing change anything in the world? . . . Is my motive any different from [my mother's]? Is it not, as was hers, a performance of deeds in the expectation of praise? . . . As for the verdict of posterity, is it any more deserving of belief than a belief in heaven? . . . Is my belief in my talent any less an act of superstitious faith than my mother's belief in the power of indulgences? And, as for the ethics of my creed, how do I know that my talent justifies the sacrifices I have asked of others in its name? (*AL*, 319)

Though Brendan cannot—or will not—answer these questions, his victims readily could, and it is clear, too, that Moore has set the reader up to answer them. All the aesthetic components of this novel, including the tripartite point of view, conspire toward our ultimate rejection of the moral position Brendan has assumed at the end of the novel, a point that Moore commented upon in a recent interview: "I wanted to show that Tierney's view of art *is* flawed and it *is* selfish; he doesn't know whether he is trying to create art or trying to become famous, and the dichotomy in his own mind hasn't really been resolved. . . . I had to make a decision about [him]: it's not really important whether he is a good writer or a bad writer; what is important is his attitude to his art."[16]

In contrast to Brendan's unfeeling selfishness at his mother's death, Jane's spontaneous weeping and readiness to accept blame reflect her moral superiority over Brendan and the fact that, in respect of Mrs. Tierney, the two have in effect exchanged positions throughout their ordeal. Jane from the outset has been a somewhat more shadowy figure than Brendan and Mrs. Tierney, but I suspect this is intentional: as indicated earlier, she is essentially a very ordinary person, not at all caught up with trying to prove something, like Brendan, or trying to overcome something, like Mrs. Tierney. She simply wants to capture some purpose or meaning in a life that increasingly seems to become more empty and sterile, and Brendan's depriving her in effect of himself, her home, and her children intensifies her feelings of uselessness and isolation. From this perspective, her surrendering to her sexual fantasies reflects literally the only way she can both fulfill herself sensually and create for herself a role of usefulness, though she very quickly senses that the fulfillment is in fact more illusory than real.

In her quest, she is not unlike Judith Hearne in that she moves from a position where her illusions sustain her to one where they are shattered forever, with nothing to replace them except self-knowledge. Just as Judith in a Catholic world loses the faith that shapes and defines that world, so Jane finds that her phallic worship is ultimately insufficient in a world that in many of its aspects is essentially sexual. Unlike Judith, however, Jane can intellectualize about the nature of her world and about her position in it, and in this existential tendency she anticipates Moore's more complex heroines, like Mary Dunne and Sheila Redden, whose deliberate immersions into sexuality are, as we will see, both more healthy in their genesis and more productive in their effects.

In her basic quest for meaning, Jane moves steadily from a position characterized by selfishness, frustration, and sexual compulsion to one of a genuine understanding of both herself and others. Her initial hostility toward Mrs. Tierney, mutually generated by her own lack of charity and by the latter's ignorance, soon gives way to a cautious truce, brought on both by their being in league against Brendan and by the bond created by their suppressed sexuality, both in fantasy and in fact. Though it is Jane who in literal fact orders Mrs. Tierney out of their house, it is also she and not Brendan who goes to visit her, and her spontaneous calling her "mother" is, like the Ancient Mariner's blessing the sea-creatures "unawares," an act generated by a genuine change of heart. Alone of the three protagonists, Jane learns the meaning of love and charity; Brendan is thwarted by his compulsion for his art, Mrs. Tierney by a Calvinistic unwillingness to forgive.

Like Ibsen's Nora Helmer, Jane realizes that only a "miracle" can save her marriage, and on that crucial Sunday evening of Mrs. Tierney's death and Brendan's editorial crisis she desperately waits for the miracle to occur: that "he would meet her tonight shame-faced and repentant, tell her once and for all that he had been wrong" (*AL*, 304). Brendan's failure to do this signals the end of their relationship, and as she looks over the city in the early hours of a new day, she comes to an existential realization of the nature of her world:

For a time she sat staring at the city's red glow, feeling cheated, remembering the rag bag of articles and books she had read in the past ten years, her mind dithering among the catch phrases of her time: affluent society, beat generation, existential decision, nuclear holocaust. But somehow she could not feel that the plight of her generation could really be called tragic. Her generation was not tragic, she decided: it was pathetic. . . . She sat until the darkness faded, the red neon glow behind the buildings died in a gray milk sky. The city was no longer on fire. It seemed dead. (*AL*, 309-10)

The love she had proffered to Mrs. Tierney and to Brendan had been rejected; the lust she had expended on Vito was extinguished. Her realization that at twenty-eight there was no adult with whom she could form a relationship reflects the extreme isolation into which she has been cast; her position in limbo is a more vulnerable one than Brendan's, for he, she realized somewhat bitterly, "would be a success, she had no doubt about it. He would write more books, he would be praised, he would be a Solomon Silver all over again"

(*AL*, 308). In light of her faith, Mrs. Tierney's final section had at least ended with the positive possibilities of the frenzied question *Love me?* Jane's final vision involves a different kind of death, a death-in-life, a kind of everlasting ennui in some limbo of man's own making.

In a letter to Moore, Hugh MacLennan said that *Limbo* "may well be the most terrifying novel ever written by anyone resident of this continent. Terrifying in a way Melville was not because . . . what you have written is too intimate to be involved with myth."[17] He is not entirely correct, for *Limbo* evolves out of a mythical nexus which is as substantial and as relevant to Moore's vision as the biblical myths were to Melville. Nevertheless, the terror that MacLennan alludes to poses a singularly personal threat, for it possesses a potential to undermine the foundations of our accustomed morality, much as Sheila Redden's sudden transformation does in *The Doctor's Wife*. In this respect, though *Limbo* does not pose the metaphysical uncertainties of *Catholics* or *The Great Victorian Collection*, it is on an immediate level the most disturbing of Moore's novels to date.

IV   Fergus (*1970*)[18]

The question that Brendan Tierney asked himself in *An Answer from Limbo*, "will I be able to revenge myself on the past by transforming it into a world of words?" undergoes a further scrutiny in *Fergus*, and if the title character of this novel can be viewed as an extension of Tierney, then the answer at best continues to remain equivocal. Fergus Fadden is a more successful novelist than Brendan, but as an exile from the same kind of past, he, too, discovers that that legacy cannot easily be left behind or completely resolved. Indeed, in one sense it could be argued that in this novel the past does its best to get its revenge on Fergus, though his dismissal of his ghosts at novel's end, followed by his father's "grateful" departure, suggests at least a temporary victory for him.

In setting, *Fergus* reflects the Malibu-Los Angeles residency of its exile author, thus completing, as it were, the view from the New World which began with Ginger Coffey's Montreal. If that earlier city represented an empirically realistic and benign world where a flexible pragmatism will normally sustain even the untalented protagonist, and New York an impersonal, surrealistic, and viciously competitive arena in which genuine talent nevertheless could prevail, then California represents the logical extension of those earlier worlds: an unreal world, an ersatz world of make-believe and imitation, where substance is subordinated to appearance, talent to gesture, and, indeed, reality to fantasy. From this perspective, the hallucinatory approach that Moore adopts in *Fergus* is singularly appropriate: Fergus, along with the reader, is hard pressed at times to determine who has the most reality, the ghosts of his past or the living characters with whom he is in contact during his twenty-four-hour ordeal. It is a technique Moore had already tentatively exploited in *Mary Dunne*, and was to bring to a singularly successful level in *The Great Victorian Collection;* in *Fergus* it is not uniformly effective, perhaps because the crises that Fergus faces do not appear to be sufficiently traumatic to invest the numerous reality shifts with either the inevitability or the impact that they require.

The literal facts behind Fergus's dilemma are not unusual: at thirty-nine, living with twenty-two-year-old Dani Sinclair, he is under contract to adapt one of his two successful novels into a film script, under the direction of two Hollywood producers, Norman Redshields and Bernard Boweri. Among other things, he needs the money from this contract to pay alimony and child support to his first wife, and he is, therefore, as Boweri reminds him, "in a very soft position," but he is, like Brendan Tierney, uneasy about changing his manuscript to satisfy the popular market. As the novel opens, he has not heard from his producers for three weeks, he has just had an altercation with Dani, and thus the fit comes upon him: for the ensuing twenty-four hours or so he is visited both by a procession of ghosts from his past and by various individuals from the real world of California. In a series of scenes ranging from warm and teasing reminiscence to vicious kangaroo court proceedings, Fergus and his tormentors engage in a kind of absurd battle of wits, in which every aspect of Fergus's straying from the fold of family, church, and state is examined.

In this ordeal, the overwhelming influence of the past is reflected in the fact that its emissaries outnumber Fergus's living visitors by a four to one margin; aside from Dani, her mother, and Boweri, Fergus meets no one from his present life of any significance to him whatsoever. By contrast, family, friends, and casual acquaintances from his past literally teem in upon him, as if to remind him of the vulnerable isolation he has gained in the New World in exchange for the crowded security of the Old. And indeed, it is Fergus's own sense of his aloneness after Dani's sudden departure that brings on the first visitations:

In the silence that followed, he got out of bed, walked along the corridor, and went into the living room. He opened the glass doors and stepped out onto the terrace overlooking the sea. He stood facing the deserted beach and the waves breaking over it. And wept. (*F*, 1-2)

This is as far westward in the New World as an exile from the Old World can go, and on reaching it, he can in effect only look to himself for whatever further answers he requires. And clearly, since an individual at any point in time is the totality of what he has experienced in the past, his asking answers of himself symbolically means the calling forth of all those who have had a hand in shaping his life. Not surprisingly, therefore, though Fergus asks a lot of questions, the answers he receives are not new, for they are the answers he already knows.

But there is a further reason why the past appeals to Fergus in his present state of isolation: there is in effect no past in California, where the artifacts of civilization are all imitations of reality. Mrs. Tierney noted with alarm in *Limbo* that the Tierney sitting room "made her think of a room on a stage: it was not real. There was not one thing in it from their family homes, not one thing which looked as though it had belonged to someone else before them" (*AL*, 45). And it is the impersonal and ersatz quality of so much in California that struck Fergus when he first arrived, as he explained to his friend Dick Fowler:

". . . everything in these apartments is made of some type of synthetic material, which, if possible, is designed to look like the natural material it replaces. And these materials repel wear and tear. Stains wash off. I could live here for a year and leave no mark on anything. My presence would count for nothing." (*F*, 133)

And because "everything here is designed to deny one's existence" (*F*, 134), the only way Fergus can prove he does exist is to call upon witnesses who can attest to it.

One of the lingering ironies of this novel is that though Fergus does dismiss his ghosts of the past, he is at the end still saddled with the very real plights of his present life, and one of the novel's central questions—and perhaps weaknesses—is whether he has moved into a position where he can resolve these. In this light, *Fergus* is a more pessimistic and disturbing novel than the other two exile novels, and clearly anticipates such later works as *Catholics* and *The Great Victorian Collection* where the protagonists are similarly saddled with dilemmas whose satisfactory resolutions are impossible. Fergus's frequent asking Dani whether she loves him reflects, too, his further fear that she might also very quickly become part of his past, thus making his isolation complete.

In Moore, the longing of the exile figure for a past time and place characteristically takes the form of a lament for the father, even though fathers in his fiction are notoriously quick to write off wandering sons as irrevocable failures. This, we recall, was the situation with Daniel Kelleher and his son Michael in "Grieve for the Dear Departed" and with both Vincent Bishop and Turlough Carnahan and their fathers in "Uncle T," and most strikingly with Brendan Tierney, whose lament reflects clearly the sense of loss that he can now never overcome:

I know only that if I were granted the wish to bring back to this world for one hour any human being I have known or read of, I would put in the call tonight for my father. We would not be friends. I might be shocked at his bigotry, his vanity, his platitudes. But there, standing in the kitchen, holding his signet ring, I suddenly, desperately, wished that he were with me. I wanted to tell him that I am about to change my life. I wanted to prove to him that he was wrong, that I, of all his children, will do him honor. O Father, forgive me as I forgive you. Father, I am your son. (*AL*, 67)

It is not surprising, therefore, that Fergus's first visitor is his father, and that it is he who utters the last spoken words in the novel: "If you have not found a meaning, then your life is meaningless" (*F*, 227), a tautology which constitutes nevertheless a moral and philosophical revelation to Fergus. In between, his father appears a half-dozen times, not on any particular signal or occasion, but very much as in real life—at his wife's behest, to go to church, to lead the family in prayers, and so on. On only one of these occasions, appropriately right after the prayer session, is he completely alone with Fergus, who takes the opportunity to ask the kinds of questions that have been disturbing him ever since he deserted his family and faith: "Are you—in heaven?" "Then you are in purgatory, Daddy?" "If you are in purgatory, it means that, eventually, you will be admitted to heaven. So you must be happy about that?" (*F*, 146, 147). His father, thinking Fergus is an examiner, evades the direct questions and digresses on the word "happy" in a rambling review of his own career, and when Fergus wonders if that is as much as he can say, he answers significantly: "Not I. *You*. It is, perhaps, as much as *you* can say. . . . I'm sure that with reasonable application the meaning will become clear to you" (*F*, 150).

This reply of course reflects the dilemma of Fergus's questionings in all these confrontations, for it is only within himself that the answers reside; but it is significant that the ghosts don't ever manifest any clear supremacy over Fergus's present status. Indeed, in the scene just alluded to, Dr. Fadden very much senses his own uncertain position: his hugging of Fergus was "the hug of a person who does not want to let go" (*F*, 146). And just as Gavin Burke had noticed the fear in his father's face as his principles were shaken by the bombing of Dublin, so Fergus suddenly saw in his father "this look of uncertainty, an uncertainty which became something more somber as his father . . . , his dead father, lost in some limbo of another world, sat in that very real rocking chair" (*F*, 145). His face, Fergus noted, was "the face of a man on a dark road at night who discovers he has taken a wrong turning and is not sure anymore where he is" (*F*, 144).

Given the father-son theme which occupies a central position in Moore's fiction of exile, it is appropriate that of all the members of Fergus's family, it is only his father and his younger self who reflect these reservations and uncertainties about the Belfast values he has rejected. His mother demonstrates only maternal, not intellectual, concern for Fergus, and is given, like Gavin's mother, to the uttering of pious platitudes about the duties of children, though she and Fergus's Aunt Kate, as he realized during his dinner with Dani and her mother, "moved in this room with a presence stronger than that of the living women" (*F*, 114). Moore's juxtaposing the mother's and the aunt's increasing mortification against the blatant overtures, sexual and otherwise, of Dani's mother to get herself a part in Fergus's play makes clear, at this point at any rate, the moral bankruptcy of Hollywood. But Fergus's second sister, Kathleen, represents a side of Belfast's Calvinism that is every bit as destructive as California's hedonism:

. . . she said [her prayers] as though she meant them, head down, droning out the responses, a life of pious ejaculations, plenary indulgences, examinations of conscience. . . . Yes, the generic Irish female of the sort who kept the priest in Powers' whiskey and Ireland the most distressful country, Europe's back of beyond. Old spleen curdled in him at the thought of her and what she had become. (*F*, 141)

It is only Fergus's older sister, Maeve, who is critical in a constructive sense, and throughout his entire ordeal, like Gavin's sister, Kathy, she is both his comfort and in a sense his conscience. Rejecting Fergus's disclaimer of any interest in the afterlife, Maeve poses the same kind of question that disturbed Brendan Tierney:

"No? Then why do you worry about your so-called literary reputation? I'll tell you why. Because, in your case, it's a substitute for belief. . . . As a Catholic, you were brought up to believe in a life after death. But you can't believe in it. So you invent a substitute. You start worrying about your reputation outliving you. Your work becomes your chance to cheat the grave. That's a very attractive thought, particularly for ex-Catholics. That's why you care so much about your literary status." (F, 54-55)

Though she is from the world of the living rather than, like the parents and aunts, from the world of the dead, she has much the same kind of advice for Fergus, but of all the visitors only she articulates what the others leave implicit: "Don't you realize I can't tell you anything? You have to find out for yourself" (F, 56).

Fergus—along with the reader—is never quite sure what it is that he wants to find out, and many of his minor confrontations do little more than repeat harmless childhood experiences. He has his youthful suspicions confirmed that Father Kinneally in his self-appointed censor's role took the scissors to the brassiere ads in the school dentist's magazines; his masturbatory recollections of Mrs. Findlater (ironically, the dentist's wife!) are given to us in instant replay as she materializes on the chaise lounge; and he revenges every schoolboy in *Lupercal* by administering a sound caning to the Reverend Daniel Keogh, though his aroused sadism while doing so makes him fear he might be as bad as his former tormentors. But running through many of the other confrontations is the theme of personal betrayal that gives a tangible dimension to Fergus's symbolic betrayal of family, church, and state, and these betrayals invariably involve women. There is Peggy Sanford, the girl he was supposed to marry—"that person he did not speak of, the one he hoped never to meet again" (F, 109), thus for the moment assuming the persona of the revengeful narrator of "Preliminary Pages for a Work of Revenge":

I am that person you insulted. I am that person you forgot. I am the one you do not speak of, the person you hope never to meet again. . . . I am that person you betrayed. I am the one who confided my faults, my shames,

my fears. I am the the one to whom you swore secrecy, whose confidences
you promised to respect.

He is momentarily disturbed, too, by a group of three women who,
by their malicious sniggering, appear to be in collusion against him,
women who played progressively more complex sexual roles in his
life—his first date, his first seduction, and his first wife. Like a
portrait by Edvard Munch, they sat, "their backs to him, their knees
hunched up, staring at the breaking, phosphorescence-tinged
waves" (*F*, 187); by carefully reconstructing in his mind what they
were really like, however, he is able to dismiss them, for "he could
think of nothing he might say to them" (*F*, 187).

But the most disturbing betrayal is one which involves no obvious
self-interest on the part of Fergus at all, or any deliberate attempt to
forget, as was the case with Peggy Sanford. And that this part of
Fergus's ordeal takes up the final forty or so pages of this novel
suggests something extraordinary in Fergus's inability to recall the
name of a girl who was in every sense quintessentially ordinary. It is
an exercise in which he is threatened by the mob, harangued by the
priest, and prompted by his family in an absurd Twenty Questions
game, and which, unpredictably, he solves only when he is alone
with her and suddenly identifies her when she "gave a small,
theatrical sigh, and that sigh, seemingly inconsequential, was the
thing he remembered" (*F*, 219). Fergus tries desperately to rationalize his forgetfulness in face of the frenzied charges of the mob:

"Look. Let me try to explain? Most people live their lives in one place, and
they meet, essentially, the same people, year after year. But I've lived in
Ireland, worked as a newspaperman in England and France, came to
America and worked on Long Island, then in New York, and now I'm here
on the Pacific, I'm trying to say I've lived in so many places, it's impossible
to remember—" (*F*, 200-201)

His bewilderment at the mob's charges of his selfishness toward
Elaine is ultimately vindicated, for, as it turns out, he has only
performed good deeds in her life: he introduced her to her future
husband, he was best man at their wedding, and he became
godfather to their daughter. But nevertheless, there was a kind of
selfishness operating here, in that his good deeds contributed to
their stature rather than his, and for that reason they were expunged
from his memory. "I don't know how you forgot us," Elaine chides

Fergus. "I suppose you meant more to us than we meant to you" (*F*, 220), and Fergus realizes along with Mary Dunne the relationship between indifference or selfishness and hell.

This lengthy beach scene clearly is meant to signify more than Fergus's casual forgetting and remembering of Elaine, an outcome that is somewhat anticlimactic in view of the ordeal Fergus has just gone through. It is one weakness of this concluding section of the novel that the relationship between his recognition scene and the other tendencies suggested by the components of this episode is not made clear. The mob's ugly, threatening mood, Father Allen's vicious diatribes against Fergus, Fergus's sudden, near-fatal heart attack: all these appear to have only a peripheral relationship to his recognition of Elaine. The mob, it should be noted, is as hostile toward Elaine as it is toward Fergus, though she has committed no greater transgression than being from the New World rather than from Belfast, which of course, in light of Father Allen's distortions, is crime enough. Clearly, the moral superiority resides here in Fergus and Elaine over their Old World counterparts; Father Allen seems to represent the culmination of the worst elements of rigid, uncharitable Catholicism first made visible in *Judith Hearne*'s Father Quigley, and cropping up later in the recollections of Ginger Coffey and Gavin Burke.

But the connection between Elaine's appearance, identification, and disappearance on the one hand and, on the other, Fergus's heart attack, revival, and resolution with his family is perhaps more symmetrical than it is organic. Clearly it is the sudden end of his entire ordeal rather than Elaine's dissolution into thin air that brings on his attack, and there is a fitting irony in the fact that Fergus almost enters the realm whence his ghostly visitors came. Appropriately, too, the father revives the son by his presence, ministers unto him by his prescriptions, and gives an ambiguous answer to Fergus's lingering doubts about an afterlife: "We have to live and die here" (*F*, 226), but, significantly, he adds that "faith and belief, yes, I had those things in my life" (*F*, 227).

In both a literal and a symbolic sense, all that Fergus has gained from his father at this point is a continuation of his present life, and thus the celebration of his "birthday" during this episode is appropriate; whether he will subscribe to some sort of "faith and belief" is a debatable point. In one sense he has arrived at the point that Yeats's Fergus reached in his dialogue with the Druid: "But now I have grown nothing, knowing all." There is clearly a measure of hope for Fergus implicit in the fact that the novel ends with the coming of dawn rather than in the kind of darkness that he had earlier seen surrounding his father. The breakers are again pounding on the shore as they were when Fergus began his lonely day, and if they are "monotonous as a heartbeat," they are of course as steady as a heartbeat as well. In this context, his earlier recollection of the line from Xenophon, "*Thalassa, Thalassa, the loud resounding sea, our great mother, Thalassa,*" takes on a new significance, for the Greek exiles who long ago sang that lament also found joy and strength, as well as sadness, in that sight far from their homeland.

Fergus derives even less comfort from his real-life visitors than he does from his ghosts, particularly from the one who at this point has complete control over his fortunes. Boweri materializes in Fergus's living-room as suddenly as the ghosts, and for the same reason: Fergus is as worried about his present as he is about his past. Boweri, the producer, and Redshields, the director, are, in contrast to the ghosts, obscenely tangible in body and mind, and Fergus has good reason to rue the day he came under their spell. "How easy it was to rationalize that first taste of corruption," Fergus remembered (*F*, 63), and his major victory by day's end is that, by failing to telephone Boweri, he severs his relationship with them, though losing his income in the process. Redshields is never present physically at Fergus's house, but the imaginary phone call Fergus makes to him assumes as much reality as any conversation in the novel; this is appropriate, for as he remembered from his one unforgettable visit, "direct conversation was, to Redshields, a secondary form of conversation. . . . The telephone was, quite simply, more real to Redshields than anything that happened outside its circuits. On it and in it and through it, he lived his life" (*F*, 30).

Fergus's confusion about the nature of the real and the unreal in California first manifested itself upon his arrival from the East, when he mistook Hank, the chauffeur, for Boweri, not surprising, perhaps, in light of the fact that "on his days off, this chauffeur drove a Lincoln Continental of his own" (*F*, 63). Both Boweri's and Redshield's houses intensified this confusion, as did their deceptive words and actions, and their vulgarity made a mockery of their charge that Fergus's writing lacked warmth and honesty. Given Fergus's involvement with these "unreal" monsters, the unreality of his mistress Dani, and, to a lesser extent, of her mother, Dusty, is appropriate. Dani is little more than the ubiquitous leggy beauty found both off and on the screen in Hollywood, and her relationship with Fergus is perhaps as inexplicable as her true nature is elusive. Fergus's sexual attraction to her is understandable, though he has to confess to himself that some of her antics "made him wonder if he overestimated her intelligence" (*F*, 101); it is perhaps appropriate that he was first attracted to her when he was discussing the ersatz qualities of Los Angeles in general.

Her mother is a far more substantial creation, reflecting Moore's characteristic success with older people whose dilemmas, though perhaps somewhat ludicrous, are nevertheless genuine. Dusty represents the faded marginal, continually on the lookout for bit parts to sustain her illusions, and in this respect she is not unlike Judith Hearne; in her brazen soliciting, however, she is the liberated New World woman brought almost to the point of caricature. The final scene where Fergus carries on a simultaneous conversation with the resurrected Paddy Donlon and the intoxicated Dusty is more than a brilliant stichomythic narrative: it links three individuals whose genuine problems are only slightly camouflaged beneath their illusory banterings. Fergus recognizes in Dusty something substantial: "Dusty can make Dani weep, Dani who never weeps. Why? Because parents form the grammar of our emotions. As mine have mine . . . " (*F*, 120).

Moore was fully aware of the aesthetic problem he faced in pursuing in this novel his most drastic departure from realism in his work up to that time. His working notes on *Fergus* record his worry about whether his "abilities as a realist [can] give the real and moving and frightening stamp to the unrealities that man lives through,"[19] and in a letter to his English editor he anticipated the problems his novel might face in North America: "As you will see, it's rather a metaphysical book, and my own idea was that it would probably be of more interest to people on your side . . . than it will be here."[20] As Moore recounted to Donald Cameron, his predictions about the public's reception of *Fergus* proved to be "crashingly accurate," but it is interesting to note that he himself has remained satisfied with both his conception and his execution of this novel—as he hasn't, for example, with *Ginger Coffey*. *Fergus* pushed him beyond what he had already competently accomplished several times, and it evolved quite logically out of his developing interest in metaphysical reality, his continuing concern for aesthetic experimentation, and, seemingly, his curiosity as to whether he had finally exorcised the ghosts of his own past.

CHAPTER 5

Metaphysical Dilemmas

I Introduction

IT took Moore well over a decade, and some half-dozen novels or so, to exhaust the fictional possibilities residing in the issues which linked his protagonists to their phenomenal world, either a fixed world predicated on the centrality of institutionalized faith, or a fluctuating world in which faith vied uncertainly and unevenly with existential impulses. In all these novels, however, even in *Mary Dunne*, where Moore experimented quite freely with time and memory, the worlds in question were totally realistic and empirically verifiable, and any intrusions of fantasy or make-believe remained unambiguously on the level of the extrarealistic. With *Fergus*, as we have seen, Moore attempted, with mixed success, something quite beyond that, in his deliberate fusing of the empirically real and the hallucinatory, thereby examining the question of reality from a metaphysical rather than from purely a psychological or sociological perspective. For the duration of his ordeal, Fergus was in effect unable, or unwilling, to distinguish between these two dimensions of his world, though his final dismissal of his ghosts suggests at least a temporary resolution of the psychological and social dilemmas which lay behind his hallucinatory manifestations in the first place.

With his next two novels of the 1970s, Moore denies his protagonists the comfort of even this temporary resolution, and in this respect *Catholics* and *The Great Victorian Collection* reflect metaphysically the bleakest of visions. Even in so despairing a novel as *An Answer from Limbo*, which many readers feel transmits the most excruciating of resolutions, Brendan acts within the dictates of free will and is therefore almost totally responsible for his own situation; Tomás O'Malley and Anthony Maloney, on the other hand, are in a sense both unwilling architects and powerless victims of their own creations. What they created in isolation through the power of belief, and sustained for a while through dedication, they are

104

ultimately unable to control as the world at large impinges upon them, and their only choice, imposed upon them by forces other than themselves, is, to use O'Malley's words, to enter a kind of "null" from which they "would never come back" (*C*, 107).

As he had done in *Fergus,* Moore in these two novels establishes the credibility of the unreal world through a precise ordering of detail that conveys the assumption of reality: everything that Fergus, Kinsella, and Maloney are seen doing as the respective novels open reflects an ordinary and verifiable universe, and leads the reader into expecting yet another manifestation of the scrupulous realism that has characterized Moore's other works. *Fergus* and *The Great Victorian Collection* in this respect require a more sudden and a far greater suspension of disbelief than does *Catholics;* hallucinations and materialized dreams are further removed from empirical reality than are the futuristic manifestations of present-day tendencies which constitute the framework of *Catholics*. But in all three novels the transition from the mundane to the unreal is achieved, as in Swift, Huxley, or Orwell, through the process of verisimilitude: one has only to accept the original, fantastic premise, and everything that follows is both predictable and convincing. That *The Great Victorian Collection* is more fantastic or unreal than *Catholics* is in large part a reflection of the widely different purposes Moore had in these novels: *Catholics* exploits and in a sense resolves the recurring concerns that Moore had always manifested over the question of institutional and private faith, whereas *The Great Victorian Collection*, his only "nonthesis" novel, is a novel about ideas in which he is completely free of the formal requirements that in part shaped his earlier fiction.

II   Catholics (1972)[1]

The only nonrealistic aspect of this short novel, published originally as a novella in *New American Review, 15*, is its chronology, for it is set in the future, just as the twentieth century is drawing to a close. What Moore might risk by selecting a futuristic setting is more than offset by the historical authenticity he achieves in terms of the consolidation of the ecumenical tendencies that were in evidence in the middle decades of this century, and given official encouragement by Vatican II in the early 1960s. And Moore further reduces his violations of realism by choosing as a physical setting a place as timeless as it is possible to find: Muck Abbey, off the Kerry coast of Southwest Ireland, where the routines of its few inhabitants have scarcely changed since the abbey was built in the thirteenth century. Out of this juxtaposition of inexorability and timelessness Moore creates a metaphysical drama which is paradoxically both an urgent invocation to "the beauty of belief" and a spare chronicle of existential despair.

Though historical and ecumenical documents validate the framework of *Catholics*, the novel also grew out of Moore's private concern over what had happened to the Church since his youth, a fact he suddenly was reminded of during a Roman Catholic service he attended in Nova Scotia in the late 1960s. In a subsequent CBC interview,[2] he said that he wrote the novel in part as a prediction: that the Church as we now know it will in effect cease to exist by the end of the twentieth century. He sees this transformation as one of the most important events of our times, for the issue then really becomes whether or not one can really believe in God and prayer. Vatican II by 1965 had pronounced unambiguously upon the necessity of Christian unity throughout the world, and upon the desirability of reunion with the Eastern churches still outside the fold; the novel assumes these goals have been achieved, for the fictional Vatican IV has now progressed to the point where serious ecumenical talks between Christian and Buddhist leaders are under way. It is this projected historical juncture which brings Kinsella to Muck Abbey, with orders "hot from Rome" for the recalcitrant Father Abbot.

"James Kinsella, Catholic Priest" is an automaton and organization man so dedicated to the new ways of the Church that he never refers to himself as "Father," except in emergencies, so to speak. In both person and deeds he in effect emerges as a virtual personification of the predictions pronounced by Pope Paul VI to the closing assembly of Vatican II:

"The Council wishes to . . . translate into brief messages and in a language accessible to all men, the 'good news' which it has for the world and which some of its most respected spokesmen are now about to pronounce in your name for the whole of humanity."[3]

The confrontation between this "spokesman" for the new order and the sixty-nine-year-old Thomás O'Malley constitutes the major dramatic tension of this novel, but the resulting dialectic is not merely the opposition of a superficial new order and a dedicated old order. Beneath the surface of the Abbot's external firmness and absolute control over his fellow monks resides an uncertain, frightened, and doubting soul who, in order to meet his dual loyalties to the Church and to his followers, must make one of the most crucial decisions of his life. How Moore resolves this dilemma takes us into the realm of the metaphysical, for we will never know whether the act of prayer the Abbot is compelled to indulge in is going to solve his problem; we only know that one year away from his allotted three score years and ten, he has made an existential commitment which will sustain his fellow monks for the short time remaining before the relentless tide of ecumenism engulfs even this remote and timeless island.

The imminent closing out of Father Abbot's seventh decade is paralleled by the drawing to a close of the twentieth century, though Moore has virtually stripped the novel's physical setting of any futuristic details in order to make the liturgical controversy relevant for all times. Indeed, the various contrivances of transportation and communication that Kinsella encounters in Cahirciveen in the opening section—the curraghs, the old monastery car, the crank-operated telephone—link us more to the end of the nineteenth century than to the beginning of the twenty-first. Even the helicopter which conveys Kinsella to the abbey in part two is hardly futuristic for the reader, though it is for the Muck Islanders: "That's the first flying machine of any description that has ever landed on Muck," the Abbot tells Kinsella. "You've brought us the symbol of the century" (*C*, 37). Aside from O'Malley's reference to closing "the hundred years out," there are, to be sure, details here and there which point to the novel's being set in the future: references to Vatican IV, the 1930s birth date of Kinsella's mother, and so on. But essentially the story, like Muck Island itself, is timeless, a point reinforced by the harmony which links together the opening image, "The fog lifted. The island was there" and the closing invocation, "Hallowed be Thy name."

Kinsella, in his grey-green fatigues and flying jacket, is the novel's most futuristic element, or, perhaps more accurately, the individual most fundamentally out of step with local time and place: not a soul he meets recognizes him as a priest. As a spokesman for the new ecumenical order, however, he is caught up in the dilemma that seems ultimately to transform all revolutionaries: they become more intolerant, rigid, and conservative than the forces they have overthrown. Governed by utilitarian concerns like "uniform posture" and "for the greater good," he is not unlike that other organization man, Bernard Hickman of *The Great Victorian Collection;* both men are more concerned with smooth management than with the human and moral dilemmas that beset their adversaries. Kinsella, a product of the liberal wing of the Church of Rome, trained by the revolutionary Father Gustav Hartmann to help bring about dissent and social action, finds himself at this last outpost of the old Church compelled to prohibit dissent; unable to muster any spiritual arguments against Father Abbot's traditional Catholic practices of Latin Masses and private confessions, he can only subdue him by a kind of military force—the serving of an "Order Plenipotentiary" carried in his "paramilitary dispatch case." Small wonder that Father Abbot's fellow monks call him "the inquisitor" or that Brother Kevin remarks that he looks "like a soldier boy."

Not the least of the ironies of this novel is that in his essential secularity Kinsella is in fact an unwitting ally of his adversary, the Abbot, who explains that he is "a sort of foreman here, a sort of manager. It is not a lot different from a secular job" (*C*, 97). But this, of course, is his characteristic understatement, for his real problem is a deep rooted spiritual malaise, a condition intensified by an early visit he had made to the shrine at Lourdes:

It was not the first time. There had been moments before . . . where, back on Muck or in some church on the mainland, that bad time had come on him, that time when, staring at the altar, he knew the hell of the metaphysicians: the hell of those deprived of God. When it came on him, he could not pray, prayers seemed false or without any meaning at all. Then his trembling began, that fear and trembling which was a sort of purgatory presaging the true hell to come, the hell of no feeling, that null, that void. (*C*, 81)

Within their realms of jurisdiction, both Kinsella and O'Malley are more concerned with the imposition of authority than with the practice of faith. "Breakdown. The loss of control," the Abbot agrees. "There must be discipline" (*C*, 64), and one is therefore not surprised at his ultimate decision to obey the ecumenical decree delivered by Kinsella from the Father-General.

He delays his decision until the next morning not for any tactical reasons, as Kinsella feared, for he knows from the start that the game is up; rather, for as much his own sake as for Kinsella's, he wants time to put his articles of faith to a kind of final test before he succumbs. In his pointed questionings and detailed explanations, in his touring Kinsella around the Monastery, in his laying on of tea and a special feast where, *mirabile dictu,* loaves and fishes *are* served—in all these ways he wants to demonstrate the meaning of faith and dedication. As one of the new breed of priests, Kinsella had never experienced a Latin Mass, and indeed, he views the Mass as purely a symbolic act; like his mentor Hartmann, he believes the Church's main business is the betterment of mankind rather than the saving of souls. Such a priest needs not only to be humored, O'Malley seems to imply, but should have at least one glimpse of what the Church of Rome used to be like before it is too late.

Of the three areas of conflict with which the Abbot has to contend—Rome, his own monks, and his own mind—the first two are, as we have seen, soluble through the same rationale: just as he must be obedient to Rome, so his monks must be obedient to him. But there is impending insurrection here, as Kinsella and Hartmann were witnesses to the earlier insurrection within the Church at large, and O'Malley finds himself compelled to resolve the third conflict— that within his mind—before he can ultimately resolve this apprehended insurrection. Up to this point, he had carefully avoided any occasion where he would publicly have to reveal his lack of faith; his permitting Father Manus to explain the Latin Mass to Kinsella is merely one more instance of his evasion of this crisis. But with Kinsella gone, and the monks clamoring for explanations, there is no further escape:

"No one can order belief," the Abbot said. "It is a gift from God." But even as he said this, said the only truth left to him, he saw in these faces that he was failing, that he was losing them, that he must do something he had never done, give something he had never given in these, his years as their Abbot. What had kept him in fear since Lourdes, must now be faced. What he feared most to do must be done. And if, in doing it, I enter null and never return, amen. My time has come. (*C,* 105)

And as he leads the monks in prayer, "his trembling increased . . . [and] he entered null," but in their echoing of his words he hears their "relieved" voices: *they* are sustained, and the universe he has created in this last outpost remains for the moment intact. There are readers who believe that the Abbot's act of prayer is the beginning of his return to a belief in God, though Moore's conception of this scene was predicated on this not happening: "As he kneels and looks at the altar and tries again to believe in the power of prayer it doesn't work for him. There is no happy ending. There is no light coming down from the altar. It just doesn't happen for the Abbot."[4]

If we evaluate *Catholics* within the perspective of how Moore has handled the question of faith throughout his fiction, then in a sense it emerges as a colossal irony: Kinsella's belief in the literal emptiness of the tabernacle, backed officially by Rome, joins with O'Malley's experiential realization of the same point, to offer a total and ultimate justification of Judith Hearne's fears that the tabernacle in Father Quigley's church *was* empty. And therefore the "daily miracle" that Father Manus celebrates—"God on the altar, in the tabernacle in the form of a wafer of bread and a chalice of wine" (*C*, 51)—never has occurred and never will occur. In its place, Manus berates Kinsella, is the new Mass, "what you have put there—singing and guitars and turning to touch your neighbor, play-acting and nonsense" (*C*, 52): a ceremony, indeed, not unlike that witnessed by Jamie Mangan at his wife's funeral in New York. Among other things, Moore's novel, too, has turned out to be prophetic: as I write this, a newspaper story records the ongoing controversy between the Vatican and a French archbishop who continues, this time beside the Grand Canal in Venice, to perform the Tridentine Mass in Latin, facing the altar, with his back to the congregation—indeed, doing the very things Kinsella was sent to put down in Cahirciveen. Liberal Catholics, more militant apparently than Kinsella, heckle the archbishop and one went so far as to tell him "to jump in the canal," but the archbishop, echoing Father Manus's words, said, "If we look around we immediately see the results of these changes, how they have affected the Church. It's been a catastrophe."[5]

Catholics, in the broadest sense of the word, is a political novel, evoking questions that go far beyond doctrinal matters. At the center of the controversy which brings O'Malley and Kinsella into confrontation are the very issues of the human condition which shape one's conscience and one's actions. It is a measure of the bleakness of Moore's vision here and of his disciplined artistry that a traditional route to salvation—prayer—can be so convincingly presented as the route to metaphysical despair and nothingness.

III   The Great Victorian Collection (*1975*)[6]

In *Fergus*, we will recall, Moore experimented with the fictional possibilities of hallucinations, with the conjunction of ordinary reality and rationally inexplicable happenings. There the insecure protagonist conjured up specific individuals and scenes from his Irish past in an attempt to resolve the chaos and despair he was experiencing in his California present. The dividing line between the real and the unreal was in that novel always clear, even though these two states of existence interrupted each other inconsistently and frequently, and when Fergus dismissed his ghosts at the end of the novel, his own position on terrestrial reality was, if not completely comfortable, at least tangible and recognizable.

In *The Great Victorian Collection,* which, incidentally, Moore embarked upon even as *Fergus* was being published, this metaphysical preoccupation receives a far more sophisticated and complex examination. On the surface, once the original extravagant premise is resolved, the novel proceeds within the strict limits of realism, for everything that Maloney does subsequent to the materialization of his dream, from his rational recounting of his dream to his growing despair and eventual suicide, is empirically verifiable and convincing. But it is the entire universe that is created or assumed around these realistic phenomena that transports us into the realm of the metaphysical and the unanswerable. Maloney's dilemma, and by extension ours, is, as he tells Vaterman, that his dream *has* come true: how does one handle a reality that no one has ever created before?

The weaving of a realistic tale upon a fantastic premise has of course long been an accepted part of our literary heritage, as works like Swift's *Gulliver's Travels* amply verify. Once Gulliver was transported to the appropriate island, as it were, the rest of his tale became quite acceptable as a realistic chronicle, and Swift made sure of that initial step by spelling out precise geographical and navigational details. Moore achieves a similar verisimilitude by providing rational and logical explanations of the very ordinary events surrounding Anthony Maloney's arrival in Carmel-by-the-Sea, of his scholarly background and interests, and of his dream with its sudden fulfillment. The trick is of course to delude the reader momentarily into the appropriate suspension of disbelief and then to reinstate him quickly and logically into the credible world which immediately follows. The dream coming true is admittedly the sticky point in this novel, but since we realize along with Maloney that "no one has ever done anything remotely like it before" (*GVC,* 11), we really cannot apply the rational explanations of reality to this "secular miracle," any more than Father Manus could to the spiritual miracles he tried to explain to Kinsella in *Catholics.*

The role of spiritual miracles has of course long occupied a prominent place in Moore's novels, for, in their own way, such

characters as Judith Hearne, Eileen Tierney, Fergus Fadden, and
Tomás O'Malley all dramatized the emptiness and terror of a world
devoid of the miraculous. Secular miracles are something else:
though it might be argued that while Diarmuid Devine could have
used one, and that Ginger Coffey, Gavin Burke, Sheila Redden, and
Jamie Mangan all experienced manifestations of such a phenomenon
in their various epiphanies, theirs were not of the metaphysical
variety that confronts Professor Maloney. Furthermore, of all these
situations, only Maloney's is in its initial manifestation completely
separated from any personal mission: his miracle had nothing to do
with his identity, his past, or his psychological or sexual maturation.

There is, however, sufficient evidence in Maloney's background
to make the nature of his miracle plausible and to establish his own
fitness to receive it; his Doctoral dissertation had been on Victorian
art and architecture, and he had once nourished a hope, quickly
quashed by his academic advisor as "impractical," of creating his
own collection of Victoriana. The form of his creation, therefore, is
not completely fortuitous, though its realization is, and Moore adds
further conviction to Maloney's involvement with it by dramatizing
the demanding commitments it imposes upon him. For it is not
merely a pleasant dream come true, but rather the emergence of a
new and somewhat frightening consciousness for Maloney, with its
own irrevocable conditions which ultimately destroy its creator.

Though *The Great Victorian Collection* is in a literal sense the
least autobiographical of all of Moore's novels, in a larger sense it is
an autobiography of himself as an artist, and a portrait of all artists
whose most extravagantly imagined works of art have come into
being. The realization of one's dream is, next to creating life itself,
the ultimate act of creation; one can shape this product without any
regard for the prior rules of a rational world, though, as Maloney
quickly discovers, the created thing immediately produces its own
rules which must not be violated. When an artist creates anything—
book, painting, sculpture, or collection—two aspects of this creation
inevitably confront each other: the product as the artist conceived
and shaped it, and the interpretations of it offered by the rest of the
world. The artist cannot change what he has created, and any
attempt to do so will debase it, but the rest of the world is really free
to do what it will to the work of art—even, Moore wryly concedes,
transform it into a kind of Disneyland, which, appropriately, is itself
an imitation of an imitation.

The whole question of the creative act and the nature of the resulting reality occupy Moore from the outset; the novel's opening paragraph establishes the uncertainty shared by Maloney and the reader alike throughout this extraordinary experience:

There is still some confusion as to when Anthony Maloney first saw the Great Victorian Collection. Can it be said that he first envisaged the Collection in his dream? Or did he create it in its entirety only when he woke up and climbed out of his bedroom window? (*GVC*, 3)

Reminiscent of Keats's lines "Was it a vision, or a waking dream? . . . Do I wake or sleep?" this passage raises similar questions about the creative imagination that the nightingale's song did for Keats. But Maloney does not drift into the imaginative state either through "a draught of vintage" or "on the viewless wings of Poesy"; instead, he "went to sleep in a normal manner and passed an uneventful night. Sometime in the early morning he awoke for a few minutes, then, falling asleep again, began to dream" (*GVC*, 5).

Such is the prosaic, unprophetic beginning of Maloney's secular miracle, and in the same plausible tone Moore moves deftly to explore the human and metaphysical implications of this phenomenon. In a sense, such an event calls out for melodrama and hyperbole, but Moore has long recognized the dramatic power of the unheightened scene and of ordinary realistic dialogue; through these low-key devices he brilliantly demonstrated how the world's multitudes quickly betray the creator of a miracle for their own ends. Moore takes this opportunity to launch a few satirical thrusts at such manipulators of present-day miracles as journalists, television types, policemen, and other guardians of public order, and a particularly clever scene involves two acknowledged experts on Victoriana, Yale's Professor Clews and London's Sir Alfred Mannings. Meeting by chance in the darkened parking lot location at the Collection and refusing to consult with one another, they start examining the items by means of flashlights, and "soon," Moore observes, "[Manning's] flashlight began crisscrossing that of Professor Clews": surely an appropriate image of unimaginative research experts feebly probing the vast darkness of their own ignorance while all the while the object of their research stands revealed to those who will see. On much the same note, Moore whimsically implies what man's response would be if a miracle suddenly *were* visited upon the world: one suspects that if Christ did return, Professor Clews would declare him to be a clever imitation of the real thing, and Bernard Hickman of Management Incorporated would promptly offer to represent Him on a cross-nation tour, promising lots of "audience potential" and "first class for [Him] and [His] party all the way" (GVC, 65).

In a way, this novel can be read as an allegory about the mutual disintegration of the artist and his art, or about the relationship between these two entities. Because a work of art is the realization of one's deepest imaginative processes, including the dream process, then everything that an artist produces not only becomes part of his own privately ordered collection, but also as a matter of course moves into the public domain. In the literal sense, therefore, *The Great Victorian Collection* can be viewed as a study of the public reception of the miracle that Maloney created out of a dream which in a real sense was simply the culminating act of a cumulative imaginative process. But, by extension, the book's more important allegorical meaning involves the public reception of a novelist's own collection of works or of an artist's collection of paintings, and the ultimate control the public can wield over the artist unless he can maintain a balanced perspective toward what he has created. What this implies is that any artist must surrender to the world that which by the final relinquishing act of the creative process properly belongs to it, while maintaining his own artistic integrity, which, like a chemical solution, is not diminished but only qualitatively modified by that surrender.

Because this is one of the realizations that Maloney cannot accept, he is ultimately destroyed by what he has created, and Moore cleverly uses the state of dreaming and waking to reveal the transformations that overtake Maloney. At the outset, dream and waking are virtually coexistent, and his total jurisdiction over his creation applies equally in both of these states. But as soon as he begins to relinquish control to various individuals—media people, Victoriana experts, Management Incorporated types—his jurisdiction remains intact only in his dream. The moment that exactly unites (or separates) dream and waking is made dramatically significant here: at the precise instant in his original dream that Maloney knows he is in charge of the Collection, he wakes up, and thus must literally not only confront what he has created, but must also turn over to the world what he has created. It is at this moment that the process of erosion begins, almost imperceptibly at first, but nevertheless inexorably, which transforms the quality of the created work and the way in which the world beholds it quite away from its original inception.

Many months after his original dream, Maloney experienced a sudden revelation about the Collection's real nature:

. . . he saw it for the first time as it really was: a fäery place, ringed around by spells and enchantments, a web of artifice as different from the reality it sought to commemorate as is a poem about spring from spring itself. (*GVC*, 176)

In part, this attitude must be construed as a product of his deep private despair, for by this time he was unable either to control his creation or to escape from it, as his frenzied trips to Los Angeles and Montreal proved to him. For while a poem about spring may not be as essential to mankind as spring itself, it can still be a remarkable artistic achievement, and of course it is for succeeding generations, as Keats poignantly reminded us, the only tangible proof that for that particular poet a spring did in fact exist. There is in a sense a conflict here between the two realities of form and content, and though a Keats poem may suffer the changing moods of the world, what it celebrates is captured and unchanging forever. Maloney's dream realized may very well go the way of Disneyland, but his dream as process will remain inviolable.

Once Moore brings the Collection into being, he has a more protracted fictional task remaining: to relate its progressive deterioration to the prevailing realism of the novel, so that the reader will be able to interpret Maloney's actions and words at a level beyond their literal meanings. As Moore indicated in a letter to his Canadian publisher, he was aware of the kinds of problems he faced in this task:

Sometimes I don't choose the books I write: they choose me. *The Great Victorian Collection* is such a book. I have been working on it since 1970, sometimes thinking it so outrageous that I would have to abandon it, but never being able to let it go. . . . I wanted to write a sort of Portrait of the Artist, a parable of the life of anyone who becomes an imaginative writer or painter. But if I let the allegory show openly, then readers will completely turn off the book.[7]

The sudden creation of the Collection in a sense is easy and uncomplicated for Maloney, for as an artist he is under no obligation to explain his aesthetic process to the world at large. It is therefore appropriate that he performed that deed as a solitary act, in the complete privacy of a dream, that is, removed from the conventional forms of reality. But as we have seen, he cannot maintain exclusive ownership of the product, as opposed to the process, of his art; and it is during this stage that we judge the relationship between Maloney the allegorical artificer and Malóney the ordinary human being caught up in ordinary personal and social dilemmas.

Maloney's transition from wonder to despair is tied not only to the progressive deterioration of the Collection itself, but also to his realization that he is unable to control it. "I used to think," he states in one of his many interviews, "that, because I dreamed up the Collection, it belonged to me. . . . But now I'm beginning to think it's the other way around. . . . If something you dream up comes to life, it stands to reason that it develops a life of its own. And now it's taken me over" (*GVC*, 194-95). But running parallel to this process are Maloney's relationships with the many individuals who have become part of his new universe, and some who emerge from his previous one, relationships which generally move from skepticism to acceptance to repudiation. Some of the individuals are peripheral but memorable, like Lieutenant Polita, "a heavy young man with a sarcastic manner, [chewing] gum disconcertingly all through Maloney's explanation as though he . . . were silently mouthing obscene words of disbelief" (*GVC*, 28). Others are almost ridiculous, like Maloney's mother, aspects of whom bring to mind Jamie Mangan's mother as well as Dusty Sinclair in *Fergus*. Though she is completely unable to understand her son's new reality, she is nevertheless drawn with a compassion that has become a hallmark of Moore's characterization.

But it is Maloney's relationship with the reporter Vaterman and his girl, Mary Ann McKelvey, which is most consistently connected with his despair and decline, though that entire narrative strain does not always satisfactorily mesh with the novel as a whole. Vaterman in particular seems to be a gratuitous intrusion, as though he is brought in merely to have Mary Ann materialize; his own dream of using the Collection story so that he can match his father's and grandfather's achievements many years earlier at Oberammergau does not sufficiently explain his appearance in the novel. Mary Ann fulfills a far more relevant function in that from the outset she becomes very much part of the Collection, both realistically and allegorically. During the early skeptical period, she alone seems to recognize the significance of what Maloney has done; later her personifying "a live Victorian girl" gives sudden life to the Collection and causes Maloney on another occasion to come to a sudden realization about the nature of his Collection:

This room is empty. No seventeen-year-old whores parade here before waistcoated gentry and Piccadilly swells. There is no life in my creation. There are no living figures. *(GVC, 123)*

So much a part of his Collection has she indeed become that, in spite of his sexual attraction to her, he is unable, during their hectic visit to Montreal, to consummate his love for her:

And so, as he was and always would be, a dreamer, this reality undid him. No longer a man and maid in those far-off wicked times, they were now equals, contestants, almost enemies. In silence they grappled on the bed and in silence, perfunctorily, preliminary, he experienced a brief moment of release. An onanistic moment, he was sure: his awkward partner seemed barely to have begun. *(GVC, 170)*

Mary Ann in a sense has been a sexually confused victim of men throughout her life: of her father, of Vaterman, and now of Maloney and the absent Victorians of the bordellos and torture chambers. And perhaps this is the aesthetic justification of the Vaterman-McKelvey strain in the first place: its subplot of repeatedly thwarted seduction attempts stands formally in counterpoint to the Collection's echoes of sexual perversions and rampant fornications. It is interesting to note, in connection with Maloney's knowledge of what is contained in his Collection, that it is not until after he meets Mary Ann that he suddenly and presciently knows about its hidden erotica, thus fulfilling the clairvoyant Dr. Fetema's prediction that "she may be of importance" *(GVC, 40)*.

Maloney's growing despair, like Tomás O'Malley's, is a meta-physical one, and he, too, undergoes a trembling before entering what he calls "a new sea of uncertainty" *(GVC, 176)*. It is only a matter of time before his dream, which changed initially from one where he descended to the Collection to guard it, to one where he sees it only via a television monitoring screen, becomes a total nightmare. His final diary entry before his suicide therefore becomes virtually predictable: *"Perhaps the way to break through is through unconsciousness itself?" (GVC,* 211). Like the Abbot, whose "my time has come" foreshadows his imminent death, Maloney chooses the uncertainty of the void over the certainty of the hell that life on earth has become. Death had not previously played a large part in Moore's fiction, though Mrs. Tierney's, Hat Bell's, and Beatrice Abbot's deaths in his novels, and Daniel Kelleher's in his short stories, all have significant effects upon other characters. Here it is the central protagonist who dies, and while Maloney's death comes in a literal sense as a shock, it is also an inevitable consequence of the dilemma he created, but for which in a sense he was not responsible.

It is this kind of paradox which transforms this otherwise prosaically told tale into a powerful and disturbing metaphysical allegory. Within this. perspective, the ubiquitous sign-carrying madman emerges as Maloney's alter ego, at once his conscience and his adversary. He can be temporarily banished, as in that crucial eighth chapter which marks the high point of Maloney's achievement and reputation, but he is back on his beat as Maloney concedes his inevitable defeat after his Montreal trip. And the madman's injunction that "God alone can create" received unwitting support from Maloney himself when, in support of Hickman's statement that materializing a dream with live people in it would constitute "a major breakthrough," he replies, "I should say it would. I would be known as God" (GVC, 71).

Not the least of this novel's strengths resides in some of its realistic aspects, for example, the detailed inventory of Victoriana that Moore clearly delights in recording. Like the guest list at Gatsby's famous parties, this catalogue of artifacts, implements, and erotica assumes almost an aesthetic justification of its own: the repeated recording of the items advances the narrative of Maloney's and, to a lesser extent, Mary Ann's progressive involvement with the Collection. Some of the phenomena recorded, like the secret room that Lord Rennishawe recounts having seen at Creechmore Castle, contain their own intriguing narrative which, like some fantastic epic simile, draws us quite away from the main story line. "I love that idea of the past on our door-step," Moore confessed in an interview, "unchangeable, irrevocable, the feeling that we can't walk away from it,"[8] and though Maloney probably wouldn't, we can certainly appreciate the irony of that last part of his remark.

The Great Victorian Collection seemed at the time of its publication to confirm new formal directions in Moore's fiction that were adumbrated as early as Mary Dunne and given more extended treatment in Fergus. And though the two succeeding novels, The Doctor's Wife and The Mangan Inheritance, for the moment, at any rate, have reversed this tendency in favor of a reaffirmation of his characteristic realism, Moore himself had made it clear that The Great Victorian Collection marked an important step in his artistry:

My thinking about the novel was changing around the time I was writing *Fergus* and although it had probably the smallest audience of all my books, I felt that I hadn't exhausted that element of fiction and I actually started to write *The Great Victorian Collection* before I began to write *Catholics*. At the time I was very afraid of the turn I was taking. I had a signature as a realistic writer who was able, let's say, to record things honestly; I could be trusted not to do anything outrageous or to tell a lie. . . .

It was something I was led into, because I have never wanted to repeat myself. I had begun this exploration of the past coming up to deal with the present in *Fergus* and I felt that I had to continue with it. *The Great Victorian Collection* seemed to be the metaphor I wanted. . . . In a way, I have my own "Collection" to escape from: if I had not changed and written these new novels I would be very much like [Maloney] . . ., caught, trapped, forced to dream the same dream, to repeat versions of *Judith Hearne*, to write those Belfast novels over and over again![9]

Thoughout his career, Moore has in a sense never repeated himself; he has frequently surprised his readers, and on occasion he has perhaps defied their expectations, and maybe even, with a novel like *The Great Victorian Collection*, deeply puzzled them. But unlike Maloney, he *has* maintained a detachment toward his work, and thus has been able to walk away from his achievement once he has delivered it to the world. His comments to his English publisher about this novel suggest the state of satisfaction that he has reached:

On the whole . . . I feel happy about this book, after publication, which is something I rarely feel. It's also a favorite of mine, and I do have hopes that it will, like the Collection, outlive its creator and over the years take on a life of its own.[10]

CHAPTER 6

Discoveries of Self

I *Introduction*

THROUGHOUT his fiction, Moore's recurring concern with the suppressed individual, with the exile, with the character caught between the dictates of faith and the impulses of conscience, can be viewed as manifestations of the theme of identity. In the early novels, of course, the protagonist was so completely subordinated to the dictates of various institutionalized forces that the question of identity never really arose. The idea of serious self-introspection never really occurred to Judith or Devine; in their view, it was the world that was at fault in its failure to accord them appropriate social status. And though Gavin's world was not nearly as fixed as Judith's or Dev's, his quest was not identity so much as it was the asssumption, if not of instant manhood, then certainly of a rebellious adolescence which would allow him to dismiss his father's world and values.

It was only when Moore's protagonists found themselves in a world in which prescribed roles no longer worked that they began intuitively to associate survival with the defining of self, or perhaps more accurately, to think seriously about themselves when their conditioned moves failed to produce the anticipated results. The institutions and forces in their backgrounds still wielded a residual influence, but increasingly from Ginger to Fergus, as we saw, the assumption of a new, even though disturbing, identity became mandatory. In general, however, with most of Moore's early characters, such concerns as defeat, survival, accommodation, and triumph all weigh more heavily in their final resolutions than does any proclamation of a viable self, though certainly, with Gavin and Ginger, this latter realization is very much part of their final vision.

In the novels dealt with in this chapter, however, the search for identity constitutes the central rather than a peripheral concern: all things that Mary Dunne, Sheila Redden, and Jamie Mangan do are deliberately undertaken with a view to enhancing, transforming, or discovering who they really are. These three protagonists have at the outset a clear, and to the world at large a respectable, social and marital identity which was, ironically, precisely the kind of identity so desperately sought by Judith and Dev. For these later protagonists, however, this kind of identity creates, rather than resolves, problems, and this situation is only in part a manifestation of social comfort or complacency. The more fundamental impulse is a kind of metaphysical ennui which not only occasions doubts and uncertainties about the nature of existence, but also raises the empirical question of whether one's separate identity becomes a prerequisite to the solving of that large problem. The evidence produced in this quest by Mary, Sheila, and Jamie suggests an affirmative answer to this question, but their respective existential decisions subsequently taken reflect the fact that any ultimate resolutions arrived at will not be easy or comfortable.

In his examination of this question, Moore draws upon his experiences from a half-dozen countries and upon his observations of social structures ranging from the primitive and the provincial to the cosmopolitan and the international. Within this very broad perspective, the only pattern that is visible is the predictable one that the question of identity appears to increase in complexity in proportion to the sophistication of the social order being observed: certainly it does not seem to be a problem in Butchersville, Nova Scotia, or in Drishane, Ireland. Moore recognizes that the process of self-discovery can be as uncomplicated as a simple assertion or a subconscious realization, or as complex as a protracted introspection, and aesthetically, his approach in these three novels reflects this observation. The realisms of *The Doctor's Wife* and *The Mangan Inheritance* are appropriate to their protagonists' direct responses to their situations, for by and large their circumstances demand precipitate rather than reflective action. *Mary Dunne*, by contrast, requires a more sophisticated technique, and the modified stream-of-consciousness used there is on the whole consonant with the process of introspection that Mary finds herself undergoing. That the most realistic of the three, *The Doctor's Wife*, is also psychologically the most disturbing, is a tribute to Moore's ability to invest that standard and often-maligned aesthetic with freshness and power.

II   I Am Mary Dunne (1968)[1]

The first novel to derive totally from Moore's North American experiences, *Mary Dunne* also reflects his first attempt to break radically with the essentials of realism, imposed both by the subject matter of his earlier novels and by a vision in large part shaped by his recollections of a predictable world. Mary's world is of course not the "unreal" one that shaped Fergus or Maloney, for the separate events which operate upon her during her decisive day belong very much to the world of empirical reality: hairdressers, apartment seekers, luncheons, and so on. If *Mary Dunne* represents a break from the realism of his earlier novels, it does so in the sense that Proust reflects a break from Balzac, or Faulkner from Dreiser: it is in the recollection of an experience rather than in the experience itself that its true significance resides.

In one sense, with *Mary Dunne* Moore has come full circle from *Judith Hearne*, for again he is occupied with the problems of a woman whom society has essentially relegated to a position of loneliness and vulnerability. But his working title here, "A Woman of No Identity," reflects the very different concerns Moore explores in this later novel; in spite of her sexual and social emancipation, or her material security, all of which eluded Judith, Mary is beset by a problem which is more pervasive and more representative than Judith's: the threats to her feminine identity which emanate from a world ordered by and for man. This is not, as we will see, the precise problem faced by Sheila Redden or merely the reverse of that faced by Jamie Mangan, though all three protagonists share at times common dilemmas. Its solution involves more than a sexual or a role fulfillment, goals which society can generally accept; what society finds more difficult to do is to alter its *perception* of a woman's identity aside from her sexual or social functions, and it is this dilemma that besets Mary.

Moore has explained at some length the kinds of problems he tried to resolve in his exploration of Mary's situation, in which he essentially arrives at Flaubert's *"Madame Bovary, C'est Moi"* stance:

I am Mary Dunne because I have taken my own life and transmogrified it into hers. I have taken my years of wandering from country to country, my changes of nationality, my forgettings, rememberings, my feelings of being lost and a stranger and have, I hope, made them hers. . . . [Like] an actor going onstage, like a medium trying to induce a trance, I have tried to think myself into the skin and into the mind of a young, troubled, pretty woman. And, like a medium speaking in the voice of another person, I have written the book in the first person singular, in her voice, the voice of Mary Dunne.

I do not know yet if I have succeeded, but if I *have*, the book will be Mary Dunne's autobiography, not my novel. The author will be Mary Dunne, not Brian Moore, for the voice which speaks to the reader is her voice, not mine and if the book is right . . . , the fact that I, a man, wrote it will be forgotten by my readers. . . . In my two years of imagining and writing *I Am Mary Dunne*, I became Mary Dunne. And, if I have found her voice, then I have found my own.[2]

On the whole, Moore succeeds in rendering the feminine psyche here without any sense of awkwardness, and by adopting a woman's point of view he avoids the temptation to create a man's version of what a woman should be. Furthermore, by making the action retrospective rather than concurrent, he shifts the emphasis from Mary as a fixed character to Mary's dilemmas; she in turn becomes convincing because we see her being shaped as her dilemmas unfold, and at no time are we presented with a complete, idealized, or distorted portrait.

The actual events of this particular Thursday cover just over twelve hours, from Mary's hairdresser appointment at 11:30 A.M. to her midnight contemplation of suicide and eventual resolution. And during that period, she undergoes some twelve or fifteen experiences, some trivial, some disturbing, which, as she contemplates them in her midnight premenstrual tension, assume overriding and ominous significances, and evoke confused recollections of her past, so that the very question of whether she has an identity is put in doubt. Her resulting mission, to "remember every single thought, word, and deed that happened to [her] today" (*MD*, 4), in fact constitutes her final act of her day, and in his effective exploitation of this tripartite relationship, Moore reflects not only an assured fictional talent, but a convincing grasp as well of the philosophical and psychological aspects of reality.

Mary's methodical reordering of her past is a process deriving from a philosophical speculation she had first adumbrated at the age of fifteen in a Catholic convent school in Nova Scotia. In a restatement of the Cartesian thesis, she had on that occasion wondered whether it was not more appropriate to say "*memento ergo sum:* I remember, therefore I am," for she felt that it was the act of remembering that bestows identity or substance to people or events. Now, seventeen years and three marriages later, she puts this process to the test, and the solipsistic nature of her dilemma is reflected by the fact that her first fear is that even now she is "beginning to die because some future one cannot keep [her] in mind" (*MD*, 3).

In her juxtaposition of past and present, current happenings and personalities remain indecisive in terms of their significance at the moment, even though they are, as in the case of the incredible luncheon scene with Janice Sloane, brilliantly drawn in actuality, for they have not as yet been incorporated into any pattern of memory which bestows significance upon events. Thus Mary's third husband, Terence Lavery, emerges with far less distinctiveness than either Jimmy Phelan or Hat Bell, even though he is currently a very positive force in her life; that she cannot at this point objectively evaluate him suggests that we can live with the present only because we do *not* evaluate it in the same way we do our past. There is, nevertheless, a strong suggestion that Terence will never evoke the fears and doubts of Mary's past in the way that Janice and Ernest Truelove do, for they constantly relive the past whereas Terence, as Mary observes, "wasn't interested in that, that's the past, and he never thinks of the past" (*MD*, 151). Thus it is possible that Mary's resolution of her fears represents more than a temporary equilibrium; in her rejection not only of the friendship of Janice and Ernest but also of their accusations, she clearly opts for the possibilities of the present which, as symbolized by Terence, should pose no threat to her.

This past-present juxtaposition operates as a structural pattern in the novel, in that the three or four main events which precipitate Mary's reconstruction of her past are numerically counterbalanced by those which have only a present import. The letter she receives from Nova Scotia on the one hand communicates a tangible fact, that of her mother's impending operation to remove a rectal polyp; but its main effect is to arouse Mary's sexual guilt and confusion, evoking as it does her brother's bluntly informing her "that Daddy died screwing, that some woman was in bed with him" (*MD*, 15), and her recollection of how this news has distorted her perception of her own sexuality:

I wonder has he any idea how that ugly little story has affected my life, how all through my teens, any time a boy made a pass, I froze, afraid that I might become like my father. And sometimes when I'm with people like Janice I see her looking at me and know she's thinking I'm promiscuous, and I have this foolish desire to tell her I'm not, I am promiscuous only in my dreams, those doom dreams where I am naked in hotel rooms with naked men and I know those dreams are mixed up in my mind with the story Dick told me. . . . (*MD*, 15)

Mary's mother remains throughout the day as a voice from a world that is ordinary and normal, a world where problems are real and tangible: rectal polyps in Butchersville, Nova Scotia, are somehow more substantial than paranoia in New York. But more significantly, in terms of her identity, Mary builds up her crescendo of affirmation at the end on the fact that she is her mother's daughter, thus seemingly having exorcised the sexual guilt associated with her father.

Her mother therefore remains as a creative element in Mary's reenactment of her past; the other two actors in this drama, Janice and Ernest, increasingly become destructive components, and in them Moore has presented two of the more memorable boors in Canadian fiction. On one level, Moore seems to be using these two in order to criticize his erstwhile countrymen: "My God," thinks Mary, as Janice ogles some men in the restaurant, "we Canadians are always going on about Americans, how loud and show-offy they are, but what about this?" (*MD*, 43). And later, Mary is somewhat embarrassed at Janice's gauche staring and gushing at a girl who turns out to be Julie Harris, "whose hair and costume," Mary muses, "might cause stares some places but not here"; ironically, however, Mary must have stared too, for it is she who gives Miss Harris's sartorial inventory: "shortskirted dress of yellow wool, long white jacquard stockings, and white Courrèges boots" (*MD*, 81). Ernest particularly, "a large lumpish man, very Canadian square, in his navy blazer, white shirt, maroon tie, flannels, and sensible black brogues" (*MD*, 167-68), becomes almost a grotesque version of the Canadian type seen earlier in *Ginger Coffey's* Gerry Grosvenor, but Moore saves him from becoming merely a caricature by adding a credible touch of humanity just when we are ready to give him up.

The chief function of these two individuals, however, is to serve as reflectors through which Mary's past can assume tangible shape and meaning, and it is their insensitive evocation of a number of past events that drives Mary dangerously close to a breakdown. In both cases, it is Mary's guilt over the death of Hat that is intensified: she suddenly knows during the luncheon that it was Janice who told Hat of her affair with Terence, and Ernest leaves the double implication that Hat had committed suicide and that Mary was largely responsible. The proof of this, however, is forever lost, in a letter from Hat which Mary has never received. This new dimension added to Mary's past, a "letter [which] didn't exist . . . until Ernie brought it up" (*MD*, 204), constitutes an interesting variation of the *memento ergo sum* thesis, in that an incident whose existence she never suspected suddenly becomes a very real part of her. Philosophically, this notion—*it exists, therefore I am*—may not be particularly valid, but psychologically its significance is immense. It is only the existence of a more tangible present in Terence that saves Mary from this potentially disastrous threat to her equilibrium, and which ultimately allows her to reject her guilt for Hat's death.

Both Janice and Ernest are more complex than an initial reading suggests, and are not simply the gauche Canadian tourists envious of their former friend's success and happiness. Ernie's devotion to Mary, though somewhat embarrassing, is understandable, and his breakdown as he pleads for a return of a feeling which existed only for him dramatizes the sensitivity with which Moore feels this very human predicament. As with Elaine Rosen in *Fergus*, Ernest illustrates in a sense the victim of distortion, of how we fail to see others as they see themselves, of how in the drama of our own lives, we are always the central character though we are peripheral indeed in the lives of others. Janice's motives are neither so innocent nor so noble as Ernest's, and though her viciousness and revenge-seeking are in part generated by her own problem of a philandering husband, they seem to be more a manifestation of her envy of what she regards as Mary's sexual promiscuity, and of her indignation that "the un-Virgin Mary" gets away with it. In large part, too, her feelings reflect the frustration of a person who is essentially petty and limited, a person whose real obsession is hardwood floors. As was the case with Elaine Rosen, both Ernest and Janice are manifestations of the nameless narrator of Moore's "revenge" sketch referred to earlier:

Unlike the successful friends you now court, we are not busy; we plan each visit and depend on it. Perhaps you *did* forget our appointment. Perhaps you *were* out. But then, if you really forgot, is that not a far greater wrong?

And Mary's earlier recollection of a theory that "the main crime of the Auschwitz camp guards was not sadism; it was indifference"

(*MD*, 8) very clearly has an applicability to her relationships with these individuals out of her past.

Juxtaposed against her past, and against the three main events of her day which caused her to relive that past, are a number of happenings which essentially reinforce her present identity. For Mary, the question of identity is inextricably related to the sexual question, not only in terms of fulfillment in intercourse, but in terms of her status as a woman in a society which theoretically subscribes to the equality of the sexes but which in fact is male-oriented. Moore's main artistic task was therefore to dramatize the duality without seeming to champion either the cult of the orgasm, or, as it were, a Royal Commission on the Status of Women; by establishing this polarity within the consciousness of a woman who both sexually and socially appears to have succeeded, he achieves both drama and plausibility and avoids the risk of distortion or melodrama.

In one sense, the basic opposition set up in Mary is that between modern woman and primitive or timeless woman, for aside from being the quintessentially emancipated figure, she is also a primitive in the ageless functions of menstruation and sexual intercourse. It has long been known that many primitive tribes fear the power of menstruating woman, and in a very real way Mary in her state of premenstrual tension poses a threat to the world that in a social sense is threatening her. Woman as a unique biological organism is ultimately indestructible, even though woman as a social being may not be; what Mary is moving toward is a synthesis of these two sexual facets of herself so that she will no longer have to view her identity in two distinct planes.

The two seemingly discrete events which usher in Mary's calamitous day are in actual fact closely related to this duality of her identity problem. The social threat inherent in the receptionist's forgetting Mary's name is counterbalanced almost immediately by the stranger's blunt recognition of her sexual identity, and though the obscenity of his proposition offends her, its import is essentially the same as the function she demands of her husbands. In this respect she is assured that in at least one dimension she is unchanged; but compounded by her premenstrual depression, the confusion is already upon her, and by the time she returns to her apartment she has gone through all three of her married identities.

Though we cannot really separate Mary's sexual quests from other aspects of her identity, we do see that the failures of her first two marriages were precipitated by the sexual inadequacies of her

husbands. Mary is never sure just how much her own guilt contributed to Jimmy's and Hat's incompetence in bed, but that it played
a part is beyond dispute. She had used Jimmy to escape from the
dreary provincialism of Nova Scotia, and Hat to escape Jimmy, and
in both relationships the element of sham and pretense always
intruded. "I remember a tiny feeling that it hadn't been all it might
have been," she recalled about the first time Hat made love to her,
"a feeling so small, so unwelcome to my mood that night that I
dismissed it. I never should have dismissed it. . . . For the central
thing was no better than it had been with Jimmy" (*MD*, 34).

With Terence, on the other hand, Mary's sexual experiences
constitute physical and spiritual ecstasy and complete fulfillment,
and with him there is no need for her to play any kind of a role.
Sexually, Terence functions as a sort of mean between the virile but
premature Jimmy and the semiimpotent Hat, and in terms of Mary's
identity problem he stands as a resurrective force:

And now Terence came to me naked and I shook, but you held me,
Terence, you pressed me to you. . . . I was drowning but I felt your body
against mine, your body that fits mine as no other body ever did . . . and I
knew I would not drown, for with you, naked is make it new, there is no
past, you are my resurrection and my life . . . and now Terence maketh me
to lie down in green pastures, he restoreth me. . . . (*MD*, 160)

Like Sheila Redden in *The Doctor's Wife*, Mary attains a "state
of grace" after sexual intercourse, and like her, too, she evokes her
sexual fantasies and recollections in language which is both erotic
and clinical, underscoring her compulsion to face up bluntly to the
components of both sexual failure and sexual fulfillment. The
emphasis in these recollections is frequently upon her own naked-
ness, upon the male genitalia, upon the sexual act, or upon
autoeroticism; this obsession stems not from any prurient streak
within herself, but from her realization that a frank and honest
sexual elationship is a prerequisite to the fulfillment of the other
aspects of marriage, not the least of which is the establishment of
herself as a distinct and viable quantity within that relationship. By
the end of her day Mary has moved most of the way toward the
realization of the basic sexual function of her being, a process which
her imminent menstrual flow will bring to completion. Terence's
love-making not only completes the literal obligation inherent in
the stranger's blunt declaration to Mary earlier in the day, but in its

unselfishness and fullness transforms that biological act into a spiritual experience; each occasion of intercourse with Terence is in effect a rebirth for her. Her affirmation that she is Mary Dunne, therefore, is both existential and symbolic: Mary's celebration of his love-making in terms like "make it new, there is no past, you are my resurrection" allows her in a sense to cancel out the sexual and social accretions produced by her marriages to Jimmy and Hat, and to reattain the state of innocence she enjoyed as Mary Dunne.

The other aspect of her sexual identity, however, she does not attain with as much conclusiveness. "You can't fight male solidarity" (*MD*, 7), Mary observes early in her day, and though she wins a few minor skirmishes, her realization that she is still regarded as a nonentity, even in the ideal relationship she enjoys with Terence, contributes to her instability:

Perhaps part of my uncertainty about who I am these days is because . . . I am introduced to everybody as Mrs. Terence Lavery. . . . I suppose men still look at me, but . . . when they hear who I am they at once ask if Terence is with me and what he's doing these days. Then we talk about Terence. (*MD*, 113)

As Moore makes clear in *The Mangan Inheritance*, this diminution of one spouse in relation to the other is perhaps more social than it is sexual; Jamie Mangan, too, is an appendage of *his* spouse, the successful Beatrice Abbot. Mary's resentment, however, stems not from petulant envy on her part, but rather from her belief that her sex is normally compelled to play a subservient and debasing role in society. "I hate being a woman," she asserts, "I hate this sickening female role-playing, I mean the silly degradation of playing pander and whore in the presentation of my face and figure in a man's world" (*MD*, 31). In her paranoiac state, Mary tends to exaggerate the threat posed by a number of men who briefly enter her life that day, and even the portraits of great men in Terence's studio assume an ominous significance: "from the wall, Dostoevski, bearded like a Bible elder, stared down at me in contempt. . . . Proust saw through me with calm ellipsoidal orbs. Yeats . . . ignored me to contemplate some pure beauty I would never be. All were men, all men judged me, all men were unfair . . ." (*MD*, 154). Thinking of the man who had obscenely propositioned her, Mary concluded that his real crime was "that to him women were not human like himself, but simply objects he wanted to penetrate and hurt" (*MD*, 8). Moore clearly could find much sociological evidence to justify the feminist points of view Mary conveys in these situations; the power of her assertions, however, resides in the way Moore has transformed this social reality into credible psychological manifestations of a woman who is at once a representative of her sex and a unique individual.

In the long passage quoted near the beginning of this chapter, Moore touches on the relationship between his own exile and the defining of one's identity; the question that arises from this is the one he explored initially in *Ginger Coffey* and pursued more fully in *Limbo* and *Fergus:* what course does an individual follow in a society that is not institution-oriented, and to what does a socially emancipated individual relate his quest for identity? A later novel like *The Doctor's Wife* makes it clear that the answer is not to be found in returning to an authoritarian world like Belfast, and *The Mangan Inheritance*, like *Limbo*, suggests the pitfalls to be found in pursuing an exclusively solipsistic obsession.

Mary Dunne, because of its exclusion of the Old World, dramatizes the complexities of these questions in less simplistic fashion, and for that reason gains a quiet authority and convincing resolution. Its structural movements of fusion, synthesis, and reconciliation produce in effect an answer to the question posed in the novel's epigraph from Yeats's "Among School Children": if one reconciles opposing imperatives and consciously recreates one's life on the basis of unselfishness and honest introspection, then it becomes impossible to "know the dancer from the dance." Just as there cannot be a dancer without a dance, or vice versa, for they totally define each other, so Mary assumes the permanently protean form of all dancers, and becomes, as John Wilson Foster correctly points out, "the changeling she fears herself to be."[3]

III   The Doctor's Wife (1976)[4]

In the "Work and Publishing Diary, 1955" for *Judith Hearne*,[5] the following entry appears, dated September 7, 1955: "X Day and notes—novel older woman-young man affair," and from then until October 2, the daily entries reflect both a perseverance and an apparent frustration with this novel: "X Day Novel," "Began writing Chapter I," "Novel X," "Novel Chapter I," "Novel Chapter I Recast," and so on. Abruptly, the October 3 entry announces decisively the start of *Lupercal:* "Began book as Mr. Devine Ch. I," which then proceeds without interruption and with steady progress for the balance of the year. By this time, *Judith Hearne* had been published in both England and Canada, and the deadlines had been met for the two pulp novels Moore was occupied with, *This Gun for Gloria* and *Intent to Kill;* it seems clear, therefore, that the entries cited above refer to an early attempt at *The Doctor's Wife,* which for various reasons Moore found himself unable to proceed with at that time.

That this novel had been in his mind for a number of years Moore conceded during a 1976 CBC interview, where he also elaborated on the genesis of the novel:

I have always wanted to write a love story . . . and the story of this book is based on a reversal, in a sense, of an experience that happened to me when I first came to Canada. I fell in love with an older woman and followed her to Canada actually, and in my present novel . . . she is the Irish person and he is the trans-Atlantic person, so I reversed the roles of the two characters. That was one reason I wanted to write the book, but . . . I wanted also to explore perhaps further the breakdown of values . . . which I think is not confined simply to Northern Ireland but is fairly general in Western European and . . . in American society today.[6]

The Doctor's Wife unfolds against the backdrop of a social order which in a literal sense has become not only more destructive than we remember it from *Judith Hearne* and *Lupercal,* but also more hopeless: a total political and spiritual chaos, foreshadowed by Moore in his documentary "Bloody Ulster," has superseded the rigid order that allowed, however pathetically, the Judiths and the Devines to survive with their illusions still in operation. Since Madden in *Judith Hearne,* no character in Moore's fiction has ever returned permanently to Ireland from other lands: the movement has all been the other way. In this respect, Ginger, Brendan, Fergus, and Sheila are all manifestations of the sociological phenomenon that Owen Deane muses upon as he arrives in London from Belfast: "This plane is full seven days a week. It's the best-paying run in the whole of the British Isles" (*DW*, 3).

At the outset, however, Sheila Redden is clearly in a different situation from these other exiles, and indeed, from all the evidence presented later, she has never given any thought to permanent emigration. In its eventual unfolding, though not in any deliberateness of planning, her situation is essentially more akin to that of Gavin Burke, in that she capitalizes on an extraneous situation to effect her ultimate resolution. And like him, she experiences a kind of ecstasy in her realization that the unexpected *coup de foudre* suddenly renders her entire Belfast upbringing irrelevant, and in terms of her personal fulfillment, makes all things possible, as it were.

Inevitably, Moore's novel will be compared to Flaubert's classic tale about another wife of a provincial doctor, but Emma Bovary's situation seems to me quite different from Sheila's, even though both engage in the dissimulation and subterfuge that adulterous relationships seemingly require. Emma, however, was bored with Charles, and experienced a pervasive spiritual malaise in her marriage, long before she launched into her affairs with Rodolphe and Léon; Sheila's discontent with Kevin, on the other hand, never manifested itself until after she met Tom, though seeing it retroactively we could argue that it was always there waiting to break out. Sheila's situation is more disturbing in that it is not a deliberately planned one, in that it is presented as one that could happen to any one at any time. Her marriage to Kevin over the previous sixteen years was not a particularly rich or satisfying one, it is true, but as sublunary marriages go, it was satisfactory; and indeed, Sheila's recollection of Kevin's sexual prowess during their first honeymoon leads her to look forward to a repeat performance, and thus sustain her for the next installment of her marriage. Emma, on the other hand, in her incompatibility with Charles, in her compulsive and desperate sexuality, and in her final emptiness, seems to me to be more akin to Jane Tierney than to Sheila, though her ultimate resolution is of course more desperate than Moore's vision allows for any of his protagonists.

Sheila also brings to mind a number of heroines in modern fiction who either temporarily or permanently desert their husbands and families in order to search for or to reassert their own identities. Maggie Vardoe in Ethel Wilson's *Swamp Angel*, Stacey Cameron in Margaret Laurence's *Fire-Dwellers*, Eva in Constance Beresford-Howe's *Book of Eve*, and Kate Brown in Doris Lessing's *Summer Before the Dark*, are all products, like Sheila, of lengthy marriages in which nothing monumental emerges as being *the* precipitating factor in their decision to leave. Maggie and Eva have carefully planned their departures, and their deliberate and circuitous journey from comfortable domestic residence to primitive seclusion where they assume a new identity underscores the irrevocability of their decisions; Stacey and Kate are both more compulsive and uncertain, and significantly, though they too experience a kind of primitive interlude, they eventually elect the certainty of what they know over the uncertainty of the void, and return to their marriages. Sheila's situation in a sense represents a synthesis of both these possibilities: she acts with the compulsiveness of the latter but with the finality of the former, decisions which are in sharp and startling contrast to the seeming ordinariness of her character.

The reader in a sense is never permitted to forget this conventional role and identity given to Sheila by the world which has nurtured and shaped her: throughout the entire novel, except for the initial mention of her in section one, she is identified by the omniscient narrator as Mrs. Redden, that is, as the doctor's wife; from this perspective the narrator clearly reflects the collective voice of a society that is incapable of comprehending any compulsion that would lead her to reject this respectable identity. Only in the very last segment of the novel's final section, as Sheila disappears into the void of London, is that identity dropped and replaced by the impersonal "she."

In a very literal sense, therefore, her quest for identity takes her from a situation where she has a permanent and specific status to one where she blends totally into an undifferentiated world, and in this respect her resolution is far more disturbing than those achieved by either Mary Dunne or Jamie Mangan. Mary ends up accepting, among other realizations, that she is her mother's daughter, and Jamie, his father's son; and though these recognitions might as easily constitute the beginnings of new problems as solutions to the old, they do spell out a reaffirmation of the sexual and familial relationships that created their identities in the first place. Sheila's resolution, by contrast, is a shattering one, akin philosophically to that presented in *Catholics* and *The Great Victorian Collection;* like old Tomás O'Malley, Sheila too enters a kind of "null" and likely "would never come back." Near the end, as she walks away after receiving Tom's letter and her money, her last links to the people who had shaped her life, Owen stands, "waiting for her to turn, to wave, to give one last look back. But she left him as she had left all the rest, Danny, Kevin, home. No look back" (*DW*, 275).

The "no look back," followed shortly by her three readings of Tom's letter before shredding and discarding it, dramatically signal her decisive cutting off of the past, and of her rejection of the three men—husband, brother, lover—who all in their own way tried to the very end to regulate her life. In the three alternatives that these men provide—a return to her family, a refuge in Belfast, a new life in America—Sheila is never consulted, and she experiences only more subtle pressure from Peg Conway to make up her mind one way or the other. She thus finds herself always being compelled to react to a situation devised by someone else, rather than being able to make her own plans, and from this perspective, all she really can do is walk away from it all. Psychologically and philosophically, this resolution is a fitting one: she made the original decision to leave her husband, and thus the only way she can make the next decision, given her three rejections, is in a state of existential isolation. The poignancy of her situation is intensified by this manifestation of her moral integrity: though she did not initially intend to leave her husband, she *did* leave him, and she must assume totally and exclusively the consequences of this act—a position, incidentally, not unlike that dramatized by another moral novelist, Henry James, in his depiction of Isabel Archer's resolution of her disastrous marriage to Gilbert Osmond.

Both the inevitability and the irrevocability of Sheila's passage from a fixed social identity to existential anonymity are underscored by the sense of urgency that attends her relationship with Tom Lowry. The fleeting appearance of Tom's braless friend Debbie, the threatened but continually postponed arrival of her husband, Kevin, and the imminent end of Tom's charter vacation are only the outward manifestations of the real urgency that disturbs Sheila: her realization that her eleven-year majority over Tom puts her literally in a *carpe diem* situation. Within this perspective, her total and uninhibited sexual participation—aggression as well as surrender— is understandable: since she is no longer a social appendage of her husband, she can only at the moment express her identity as a total sexual being who, on an equal basis with her lover, creates and shares a new reality of sexuality and love. Symbolically, her substitute honeymoon—in the same room where she and Kevin had their first one sixteen years earlier—represents a new and innocent beginning for Sheila. And the entire Villefranche interlude takes on the nature of a kind of paradise in suspension: the sun is always shining, there are no complications, and their love is both spontaneous and guiltless.

The reasons for Sheila's anticipation of her second honeymoon with Kevin are not entirely sexual, however, though she does have erotically pleasant recollections of their earlier sexual experiences. Villefranche represents to Sheila an escape from the horrors of her present-day Ireland:

Again, she thought of herself and Kevin on that honeymoon flight, coming here to the direct opposite of the cold, rainy strands and bleak . . . boarding houses of the seaside towns at home. And now . . . Villefranche was just as she remembered it. In those sixteen years, it was Ireland that had changed. Belfast bombed and barricaded, while in Dublin new flats and American banks had spoiled the Georgian calm around Saint Stephen's Green. . . . Yet, paradoxically, here on the Riviera nothing had changed. . . . Belfast, with its ruined houses and rubbled streets, was now, to her, the alien place. Here, as she came down into this small French town, she came home to the past. . . . (*DW*, 50)

This Belfast-Villefranche polarity is reflected in the attitudes toward life held throughout their marriage by Kevin and Sheila, and even on that first honeymoon trip, her childlike delight at simply being there was shattered by his literal-mindedness and need to remain practical. In their sixteen years of marriage, Kevin never did come to understand her, and after learning of her affair he went to her room in Belfast and stared at her books, "as though he might find hidden in them some proclamation of who she really was" (*DW*, 204-205).

Unlike Mary Dunne, Sheila never really had any doubts about who she was, and any impulses toward self-assertion she has had have been dim and undirected. Like Mary, she had married originally to escape a depressing home life, but on balance, she reflects, "I haven't had such a bad life, though. Nor such a great one, either" (*DW*, 53). Indecisiveness and dilatoriness, rather than hostility or open frustration, characterize Sheila's outlook on herself and her world; vanity and narcissism are there, too, and a propensity toward harmless flirtations, tendencies which were manifested only in fantasy until, as with Jane Tierney, opportunity suddenly materializes.

Tom represents of course more than the sexual stud that Vito was for Jane, though Sheila confesses readily to Kevin that "sex is a big part of it" (*DW*, 239). On their walk through the streets of Paris, Sheila recognizes in Tom the excitement and the intellectual possibilities that were part of her own youth, and their mutually shared reminiscences of Paris constitute an initial basis for their relationship. And always, Sheila is aware of the contrast between what Tom represents and what the reality of her Belfast life is, and indeed, her unbridled delight at being with him in Paris makes her feel "as though she were a deserter from home" (*DW*, 45), against which thought is juxtaposed her recollection of her own recent involvement in the horrors of Belfast. Tom serves as both a diversion from this part of her reality and, like Terence Lavery, a personification of the priority of present experience. And like Terence, too, in his sexuality he transforms a physical act into a spiritual one that, as it did for Mary Dunne, enables Sheila to experience a kind of rebirth:

> Yet tonight, in the quiet of this moonlit room, that feeling came back to her, that pure Sunday communion peace. It filled her, shocking her, for wasn't *this* sin, here in this room, committing adultery with this boy, how could this be that same state, that pure feeling of peace? Yet it filled her, it possessed her totally. It was as though wrong were right. Her former life, her marriage, all that had gone before, now seemed to be her sin. These few days with Tom were her state of grace. She turned, went back to the bed, and lay down beside him, holding him in her arms, pressing against his warm body. She closed her eyes. I am in grace. In my state of grace. (*DW*, 101)

Sheila's affirmation here is, among other things, a verification of Devine's earlier realization that failing to sin was his sin, and it intensifies even more the futility of his pathetic attempt to attain that state within the confines of Belfast.

In a very real sense, of course, though she has attained a temporary state of grace, Sheila cannot permanently escape the realities of Belfast, for as they returned to Paris, she realized that they had "re-entered dangerous terrain, offering themselves again to the world, their enemy" (*DW*, 116). The sunshine of their paradisal interlude in Villefranche gives way to rain, the spacious, well-lit room in the Hôtel Welcome is replaced by a "dark chamber of landlord browns and institutional greens" which by itself seems like "a place of purgatorial gloom" (*DW*, 117), and almost immediately the nature of their relationship changes. For ironically, it is in this same Hôtel des Balcons, where both Sheila and Tom had once stayed on separate occasions, and the recollection of which a few days earlier had brought them closer together, that Sheila experiences her first tangible premonition that their relationship cannot last. Tom, with his single duffel bag, brings to mind Sheila's first fleeting acquaintance in Paris, the footloose Debbie with her packsack, objective correlatives of their essential independence from time and place. As she and Tom watch the passers-by she realizes that, "as always on this boulevard, the faces were young, coming annually in an endless migration from every country, every continent, to alight here once in the long journey of their lives" (*DW*, 119). She had once briefly been part of that migration, but then found herself "locked up in Ulster for four more years of her life" (*DW*, 42), and had never been able to seize that moment again. In a hypothetical letter to God, the sixty-five-year-old protagonist of Beresford-Howe's *Book of Eve* expresses the frustration produced by the kind of wasted life that Sheila realizes she has lived:

Do You realize, I wonder, what submerged identities women like me can have? How repressed and suppressed we are by a life that can give us no kind of self-expression? . . . Even You can't know what it's like to be invisible for years on end. To live locked up. Never spontaneous. Never independent. Never free, . . . because the chief duty of females, we were taught, was to practise the restraints of civilization, not explore its possibilities.[7]

In effect, it is this message, to practice appropriate restraints, that comes from Belfast, from Kevin via telephone, and from Owen in his role as emissary. Doctors both, they diagnose her situation in medical terms, quite incapable of understanding or accepting that it could simply be a case of her falling in love. For love, as Dr. Deane realizes, cannot be explained away or resolved as easily as sin could be a generation earlier, or mental illness in this generation, perhaps because love, in part, at least, is an amalgam of both these conditions. "We put up with our lives," Sheila tells Peg Conway, "we don't try to change them. I didn't realize it, until I fell in love. What I'm doing now is supposed to be selfish. It's what people used to call sinful. But I'm happy, in a way I never was before. Is that a sin?" (*DW*, 153).

The Doctor's Wife is a totally secular tale, but in none of his fiction does Moore easily discard the machinery of faith and institutional belief, and it is perhaps illuminating to consider for a moment Sheila's psychological crisis in spiritual terms. We have already seen that she attained a state of grace during her paradisal interlude in Villefranche, and within a religious perspective, only those who have received God's grace can enter purgatory to expiate their venial sins before entering the kingdom of God. It is therefore appropriate that it is during her second Paris interlude, the purgatorial stage of her crisis, that she begins to ask questions about her involvement with Tom, and what it signifies in her ultimate disposition. There is nothing spiritual about her expiatory exercises, in which she experiences everything from betrayal to physical abuse, and even the priest whom she visits after contemplating suicide offers her Camus instead of God. Yet when she visits the priest again two weeks later, she can inform him that she has made the difficult decision, that in effect she is ready to leave purgatory for whatever lies ahead, even though in her assessment of the world to her brother, she saw this as a pretty gloomy prospect: "The Protestants don't believe in Britain and the Catholics don't believe in God. And none of us believes in the future" (DW, 182).

Of course, if she really believed that, she would have to come back to Camus, for then suicide would be the only important philosophical and personal question. But her own simple diagnosis that she is in love sustains her, and allows her to enter whatever world she is prepared to create for herself. It is fitting that she chooses neither the world that shaped her nor the world in which she made the break from her past, but rather cosmopolitan London, a kind of universal metropolis where she can both submerge herself and start an entirely new life. Though in her purgatorial state in Paris she made the crucial decision about her life, she still has penance more to do, as it were, in this final world, for her betrayal of Tom: "She thought of him constantly. She knew that some day she would no longer think of him all the time. But it had not happened yet" (DW, 270). Her discarding of his letter constitutes a necessary step in this process, but her lonely suffering will clearly continue indefinitely; her recurring jealous and erotic dreams in which Tom makes love to a young girl assume a cruel rationale in this respect, as Owen notices that "something [about her face] had changed. He could not say, exactly, but she looked older" (DW, 272). Moore clearly does not coddle his readers, and I suspect that this may well be the kind of ending that Boweri wanted Fergus to change in his novel: "I keep telling you we need some hope. Some little lift so's the audience can walk out, they don't want to commit suicide" (F, 72).

Aesthetically, however, the conclusion of The Doctor's Wife is satisfying, resolving as it does the mystery and loose ends posed by the opening prologue. That prologue—not numerically part of the novel's tripartite structure—arouses suspense and interest in that the two main protagonists exist there only as names on a letter, and even upon subsequent readings its impact upon the reader remains strong. In the final section that letter completes its journey, and while it communicates nothing new to Sheila, it fills in all the gaps for the reader; we cannot help thinking here of the unread letter Hat had sent to Mary Dunne, and how it might have filled in the gaps for her. In the prologue, the undeliverable letter signals the fact of Sheila's disappearance; the delivered, thrice-read, and discarded letter in the closing section allows the reader to witness her actual disappearing, and the novel thus satisfactorily resolves the premises on which it began.

In the course of discarding her past and attaining a new perspective toward herself as an independent and self-sufficient being, Sheila is neither so methodical nor so obsessed as Mary Dunne was. Mary's two major worries, her biological identity and her societally imposed identity, are in a sense never in question with Sheila, and indeed, her social identity as Mrs. Redden still attaches to her as she works in the London laundromat. What troubles her is not a wasted identity but a wasted life: a dull provincial upbringing which she in practical terms tried to escape by entering into a dull, provincial marriage, and Owen recollects as he returns to Belfast from Paris the regrets she expressed on this point:

"Kevin used to tell me that life wasn't all dancing in the dark. . . . He said I was impractical, that I never faced facts. He was wrong. If I'd been impractical, I'd never have married him. I'd have gone off to London or Paris and tried for a job, no matter how impractical that sounds. If I'd been romantic I would have tried for a different life. . . . That's what I blame myself for now. I didn't try." (*DW*, 190)

There is evidence of course that during her sixteen years of marriage her romantic impulses remained strong, such as her compulsive flirtations and her escape into books, but on the whole Kevin's surprise and shock at Sheila's sudden desertion are understandable: a second honeymoon in which he is suddenly not needed would likely shatter the most confirmed roué, and whatever else he is, Kevin is not that. Peg Conway remembers him as "Sheila's big lump of a husband," it is true, but one who brought some fun to their lives, and indeed, Sheila's recollection of their fun, laughter, and vigorous sex during their honeymoon suggests a not incompatible relationship. Psychologically, then, Kevin's transition from shocked spouse through cautious diagnostician to irrational rapist is convincing: his failure to understand her in his roles as husband and doctor causes him to simplify her motives into one of a sexual insatiability, which he had by and large been able to satisfy during that first honeymoon. In a real sense, his subsequent ferocious raping of her constitutes not only an ironic consummation of their long-planned second honeymoon, but also a desperate reenactment of the uninhibited sexuality Sheila had recently been experiencing with Tom. Kevin's subsequent pathetic attempt to salvage some self-respect by rushing past Sheila and Tom—because "he was going to be the one to walk out on *her*" (*DW*, 245)—reflects the extent of his frustration, as well as Moore's compassion for a man whose life has suddenly been shattered.

On one level, *The Doctor's Wife* reflects the opposite situation to that depicted in *Fergus* and *The Mangan Inheritance*, where older men are infatuated with younger women, and in that light it can be seen as a manifestation of the current "in praise of older women" syndrome. But within this formula framework it communicates a powerful moral tale, rendered all the more disturbing by its backdrop of social and moral collapse. Lessing's Kate Brown was dimly aware that her own infidelity and her husband's numerous transgressions were vaguely related to "things happening in the world, the collapse of everything, . . . [things] tugging at the shape of events;"[8] though Sheila in her celebration of her newly awakened self argues on the one hand that "you can't blame the Troubles for everything," she nevertheless proposes to Owen much the same point of view as Kate:

What do *you* believe in? Do you believe that if you live a good life here on earth you'll go to heaven? Do you believe in politics? Do you believe in trying to make this world a better place to live in? In Daddy's day, people believed in those things. The present made sense because they believed there would be a future. Nowadays, all we believe in is having a good time. (*DW*, 182)

Sheila does not entirely believe her last statement, of course, for she is essentially one of Moore's most moral characters, as evidenced by the painful way she chooses to solve her dilemma. But in desperately advancing this argument, she firmly rejects the diagnosis imposed upon her by her family and her society: in effect, she is saying, it is not lovers who are ill or unbalanced, it is the world.

IV   The Mangan Inheritance (1979)[9]

The three novels being considered in this chapter all examine, among other things, the relationship between marital separation and the search for a viable identity, and in all cases, the situation involves wives walking out on husbands: Mary leaves Jimmy and Hat, Sheila leaves Kevin, and now, in Moore's latest novel, it is Beatrice who leaves Jamie. But here, for the first time, the emphasis shifts from the person who does the walking out to the person who is left, and in this respect *The Mangan Inheritance* constitutes a continuing dramatization of Moore's compassionately held view that "nobody likes to be the one left behind," a view given poignant articulation earlier through such characters as Ginger Coffey, Ernest Truelove, and Peggy Sanford.

A large number of Moore's novels, of course, deal with the issue of infidelity or separation, though it is only in *Fergus* that it is the husband who leaves the wife. Characteristically, even when there is no overt sexual or marital relationship involved, Moore's fiction presents a veritable gallery of women who, for varying reasons and for varying periods of time, walk away from their men: Una Clarke, Veronica Coffey, Jane Tierney, Sally Shannon, Mary Phelan/Bell, Dani Sinclair, Barbara Maloney, Mary Ann McKelvey, Sheila Redden, Beatrice Abbot. Not that all these women are by any means the dominant figures; Una, Sally, Barbara, and Beatrice are little more than shadowy possibilities beside the substantial reality of the men they give up. Nevertheless, except for Una, they are in their own way responsible for the men going on to new areas of experience and assuming roles from which they are effectively excluded. Not the least of the ironies of *The Mangan Inheritance*, for example, resides in the fact that the person who took away the identity of Jamie Mangan in the first place eventually provided him with both the opportunity and the wherewithal to find himself a new one.

The Mangan Inheritance is in one sense the obverse of *Mary Dunne*, whose working title, "A Woman of No Identity," could by a simple sex change become the working title of this one. For in much the same way that Mary's identity began to erode the moment she was introduced as Mrs. Terence Lavery, Jamie, too, became little more than an appendage of Beatrice Abbot, and, indeed, even after her death, their former doorman kept calling him Mr. Abbot. This diminution of his identity began at the moment of their wedding, where the attendants and guests were all Beatrice's friends and colleagues, and as Jamie was to muse seven years later in the isolation of Quebec's Townships, "as the wedding went, so went those first years" (*MI*, 32). He sees Beatrice for the last time on

New Year's Eve, and later that night at his father's place in
Montreal, as the traditional "Auld Lang Syne" fades from the
television screen, Jamie indulges in a bitter recollection of what had
happened to them:

But auld acquaintance *had* been forgot. . . . He stared at his own vague
reflection on the dead screen. People would be kissing Beatrice, wishing her
a Happy New Year, probably saying nice things about her new romance.
She smiling her Beatrice Abbot smile, telling them how wonderful she feels,
how happy she is. Her graph goes up and up. Even when a play fails, she
gets good notices. She's a winner, one of the All-American winners. And if
she ditches you, it's because you're a loser. A Canadian loser. . . . Well,
that's over. Happy New Year. He shut his eyes and rocked to and fro on his
heels. All around him the roar of talk. "Bitch," he said softly. It was
comforting to say it. It was her fault. There was no point in pretending to
be fair about her any more. I hate her. I hate her. (*MI*, 27, 28)

Juxtaposed against their seven-year marriage is the brief six-day
period covered in part one of the novel, extending from New Year's
Eve to Beatrice's funeral ceremony the following Friday, an interval
during which Jamie in a sense is suspended between two identities.
At the moment the novel opens, he is in a state of absolute isolation
in the bare New York apartment vacated by Beatrice some three
weeks earlier; his own separated parents live on opposite sides of
the continent, his mother in a convalescent home for the mentally
disturbed in California, and his father, remarried to a youthful
Danish girl, in Montreal. Moore emphasizes Jamie's nonidentity by
drawing our attention to trivial and desultory matters—the dripping
tap, the falling snow, the professional dog-walkers below him on
East Fifty-First Street. Even the annual Christmas-card ritual that
he muses upon underscores his insignificance: he had mailed out
ninety-seven cards, and of the forty-six received, only three, including one from his mother, were for Jamie alone. In short, on this final
day of the final year of his marriage, the erosion of his identity is
complete; he is now, as he recognizes in the mirror after Beatrice's
brief and unexpected visit, merely a kind of "lifeless souvenir . . .
photographed, robbed, abandoned" (*MI*, 15, 16).

Beatrice's visit evokes another manifestation of Jamie's long
struggle for his own identity, his *poète manqué* status: in seventeen
years he has no more than two published poems and one unpublished epic poem to his credit. Both here and in a later scene in
Ireland where she materializes in hallucinatory form, her appear-

ances are accompanied by snatches of recollected verse, ranging
from Herrick to Eliot, as though he associates Beatrice with both his
aspirations and his failure as a poet. It is interesting, too, to observe
how in his exasperation and anger at Beatrice, and in his obsession
to blame her for his situation, he not only substitutes "she" for "he"
in Eliot's lines, "So he would have left/ As the soul leaves the body
torn and bruised," but also later that night in Montreal bitterly
rewords Byron's lines from "Don Juan" to suggest Beatrice's utter
indifference to his plight. And, of course, that he is ultimately to
discover the real nature of the poets from whom he is probably
descended and, more ominously, to gain some insight into his own
nature and talents, heavily underscores the irony of these poetic
confrontations with Beatrice. It is not, obviously, a happy prospect
to choose between being a *poète manqué* and a *poète maudit*, but
such, it seems, might well be Jamie's possibilities.

Nevertheless, it was his sudden realization that in effect he had
become no more than an imitation of his original self that caused
him impulsively to pursue the other inheritance:

Yet now, suddenly, he needed his father. His father might be the one
person who could help him. To his father he was his father's only son,
continuance in a line which stretched back to Ireland and their grandfather's claim to be descended from the poet Mangan himself. (*MI*, 16)

Among other things, this Montreal section of the novel quietly
dramatizes a new note in Moore, the resolution of the father-son
hostility that constituted much of the tension in such earlier novels
as *Emperor, Limbo,* and *Fergus*; here it is a mature and mutually
considerate relationship from the outset. Yet in a sense there is a
strange reversal of roles here: Jamie's marriage to Beatrice produced
only a stillborn son, while Patrick's remarriage to the youthful
Margrethe, given her pregnancy at novel's end, should ensure the
continuance of the Mangan line, which appeared to have ended
with Jamie. There is a symbolic incest motif here, too, in that both
men have been mildly attracted to each other's wife, a pattern
which, as we will see, is not only made explicit in the Irish section of
the novel, but also made part of the final resolution of Jamie's own
Mangan "inheritance," as he and Margrethe sit by his father's bed,
"watching him die" (*MI*, 336).

Jamie's instinct to return to his former home is vindicated almost
immediately upon his arrival at the airport, for "he felt, suddenly,

grateful, glad to be seen at last not as Beatrice's husband, but welcome in his father's house, a son come home" (*MI*, 18). Appropriately, however, during the remainder of that New Year's Eve, he still has to put up with the world's recognition of Beatrice's identity, as reflected by the guests at his father's party; it is not until the next day, the first day of the new year, when he begins his three-day retreat in the wilderness away from all the media that created and perpetuated her identity, that he can begin the quest for his.

In this undertaking, Jamie undergoes the two rituals necessary for its realization, a purgative reenactment of his past identity and a willing acceptance of a possibility that will lead to the new. Moore competently juxtaposes these two planes of this process so that the end of one coincides precisely with the beginning of the next one. Thus, Jamie's long reminiscence about his relationship with Beatrice is in effect a chronicle of the progressive diminution of his identity until, like Ginger Coffey, he has hit bottom. "It's as if I—the person I was—your son—the person I used to be—" he confusedly explains to his father, "it's as if there's nobody there any more. Sometimes I feel as if I'm going mad. Except that there's no me to *go* mad" (*MI*, 43).

The conversation which ensues, and which leads ultimately to the second phase of Jamie's process, is on the one hand the obligatory father-son talk that Jamie anticipated when he telephoned his father from New York in the first place, but it also reflects the dialectic of uncertainty that characterizes Jamie at this point. He offers counter-arguments and obstacles to every point his father makes about the Mangan connection, as though he instinctively fears proceeding further with this business. It is only when he discovers the daguer-reotype inscribed "(J.M. 1847?)," which bears an uncanny resemblance to himself, that he begins to believe that he is related to James Mangan, and he soon succumbs wholeheartedly to this possibility:

And in that moment, oddly gleaming under glass, the photograph stared up at him, dispelling his dread, filling him with that now-familiar sense of giddy elation. For the first time since he had watched Beatrice walk down the museum steps with her lover, he felt cured. He picked up his cure, his antidote, the face of Europe's first *poète maudit*. He stared at that face and the photograph eyes stared back, lit, it seemed, with the same unearthly excitement he now felt. . . . Giddily, he raised his glass. "To Mangan the poet," he cried. "To my resurrection. To my life!" (*MI*, 55)

That he embraces this new venture before he learns of Beatrice's death is testimony to the decisiveness with which he has severed his association with her, and evidence of the psychological growth he has experienced literally overnight. And clearly, too, we cannot miss the ironies of this situation: first, that he assumes his new identity just as her death cancels out forever any temptation he might feel to reassume his old one, and second, the exclusive role that the daguerreotype plays in his decision, in light of his rejection the previous day of his own face, which, like a daguerreotype, was "a face in stasis . . . , a waxwork countenance, lifelike, but not alive" (*MI*, 16). Nevertheless, this wilderness interlude has replaced his earlier self-pity and anguish with strength and happiness, both through his rekindled love for his father and Margrethe, and through his discoveries about his family which have enabled him to fill the void left by Beatrice's departure.

Though Beatrice's death is clearly not a requisite to Jamie's decision to pursue his quest for his identity, it does contribute a monetary dimension to the nexus of inheritances which coincide in this novel, and as we will see, allows him to be pulled further into that welter than he in retrospect would wish. It leads him, too, back to the New York scene which concludes this section of the novel, a scene of impersonal contacts, of telephones and answering services, that contrasts not only with the warmth and intimacy he had experienced during the wilderness interlude, but also with the suffocating familiarity and intrusions he is to experience in Ireland. Everything in New York, as it was for Fergus in Los Angeles, is gesture and cliché rather than substance, and nowhere is this more apparent than at Beatrice's funeral, which Mangan contrasts to his grandfather's funeral in Montreal, a man who "had died in his community [and whose] death was a part of his life":

But here, in a room which she had never seen, a room filled with flowers and greenery, with music whose tone was joyful and light, an actor had read a poem which had no significance for the dead woman it was to commemorate. Here, there was no body. No hearse waited outside to bring the mourners to a cemetery, to spaded earth at the rim of a grave. Here an audience waited for a Broadway producer to eulogize an actress. . . . (*MI*, 88)

In effect, since the woman who has given Mangan an identity in the first place now has no identity herself, since "it was the actress

who was commemorated here today, not the woman," he realizes
that it is immaterial who contributes to this charade; indeed, as the
only person at her funeral who genuinely loved her once, he is the
one who in a sense does not belong, and his departure is barely
noticed. "He was no longer Beatrice Abbot's husband, an involun-
tary hanger-on in her world," he muses. "Nor was he James
Mangan, the nineteen-year-old student whose poem had been
published in *The New Yorker*. In the years between, he had been
like Scott Fitzgerald, an indifferent caretaker of his talent, but,
unlike Fitzgerald, at thirty-six he had been given a second
chance. . . . I will go to Ireland" (*MI*, 91-92).

Jamie's pilgrimage from New York to Montreal to Ireland, a
reverse journey to Moore's own passage into exile, represents a
chronological as well as a geographical displacement, for the
southwest of Ireland emerges here as timeless as New York is hectic:

As he looked down at the fields surrounding the bay, it seemed to him that
he had gone back in time: there was a stillness in this scene as in a painting
of medieval times. The distant vista of fields, the church spire and the slate
rooftops far below, all of it was like a world long gone, still as a Poussin
landscape, unchanged and unchanging. There was no sound at all, not even
an insect's hum or a bird's cry. Caught in that stillness, he stood unmoving.
It was as though his life had stopped. (*MI*, 105)

Though the Irish section of the novel is by far the longest of the
three, it in fact covers the same number of days—six—as the first
section, but the timeless quality of Jamie's new surroundings, as
well as the confusing relationships and intrigues of the whole
Mangan clan make it difficult, and perhaps unimportant, to separate
one day from the other. The persistent gloom and rain, the
interchangeability, as it were, of night and day, provide the
appropriate atmosphere for the gothic turn that Moore gives to his
narrative in this section, though in actual fact the seemingly spooky
and supernatural phenomena derive from empirically verifiable
events and situations. Jamie soon realizes that the quest which he
had embarked upon in Canada with such elation causes only
perturbation and fear in Ireland, and though everyone in the village
of Drishane almost instantly knows everything about him, no one is
eager to reveal anything about any of the earlier Mangans. And
Jamie instinctively fears, too, after his first night in a house owned
by a member of the family that his quest "might lead him not

toward the ancestor he hoped to find, . . . but to humble relatives in this strange backward place, to people he might even be ashamed to claim as kin" (*MI*, 117).

And on the whole, the Mangans he meets in Drishane are a sorry lot: foul, greedy, drunken, and incestuous, and Jamie is drawn into this welter through his sudden lustful relationship with the eighteen-year-old Kathleen, who, he soon realizes, "was infinitely more skilled in venery than Beatrice or any other woman he had known" (*MI*, 169). This is incest far removed, it is true, and only a faint shadow of what he subsequently learns about her Uncle Michael, significantly one of the three Mangan ancestors to whom Jamie bears an exact resemblance. Another was Michael's Uncle Daniel, murdered with a meat cleaver in a drunken bar-room brawl, and of course the third one was the original *poète maudit* he had set out to search for in the first place. Thus Jamie's Mangan inheritances in this respect hardly fulfill his earlier anticipations and hopes, and in spite of his insatiable lust for Kathleen, he begins to have doubts about what he is discovering:

Kathleen Mangan, my love. Are she and her brother, and Dinny and his derelict mother, descendants of the poet, or simply people left over from another time, their speech debased, their lives mean and pointless as that of cur dogs snuffling around a trash heap? And don't I fit in, too? (*MI*, 192)

Just as it had been necessary for Jamie to remove himself from New York to the wilderness to exorcise his old identity, so from his ancestral Irish home he undertakes an obligatory pilgrimage to a ruined Norman tower to confront a tangible manifestation of his new one. His meeting with Michael Mangan not only solves a number of puzzles that had earlier disturbed him, but it startles him into a realization of his own, largely self-imposed, predicament; and he "was filled with a premonition that he was looking at what he himself might one day become" (*MI*, 307). Like the primitive who fears the photograph, as he himself had reflected upon just after Beatrice had departed on New Year's Eve, he here suddenly fears the daguerreotype that he had compulsively carried around with him: "[he was] seized irrationally by the idea that if he got rid of it now it would be a first step toward his escape from this net of unnaturally close resemblances, sordid family history, and unnerving hints of prophecy" (*MI*, 307).

He cannot of course renounce his legacy, and his fears of what he has inherited are very real: his compulsive lust for Kathleen may well derive from a propensity within him that is not all that more refined than that which drove Michael to committing incest with both his daughter and with Kathleen on earlier occasions. But he can perhaps recall the words of Kathleen's Aunt Eileen—Michael's wife—"it's what you *do* that matters"—and in this respect his earlier dialogue with the apparition of Beatrice reinforces the *mea culpa* resolution toward which he is moving. His violent outburst at Michael is in this sense an outburst against his own mediocrity, and his recognition that Michael's verse is both derivative and immoral reflects his own suddenly realized aesthetic and moral achievement. The smashing of the daguerreotype, therefore, signals the end of Jamie's romantic enlargement of himself, and of his dependence on a reality that has in large part been shaped by others rather than himself, even though he had initially succumbed enthusiastically to its possibilities.

In the course of his pilgrimage to his ancestral home, Jamie does achieve a literal solution to his quest—he *is* related to the poet Jamie Mangan—but this discovery does not produce the effects he had anticipated. And of course his father and grandfather were also related to Mangan, but they both carved out careers and identities quite removed from the legends and realities of that cursed poet, and again Eileen's pragmatic advice seems borne out. Jamie's problem becomes one of extricating himself from the situation he finds himself drawn into, and the *deus ex machina* represented by his father's sudden stroke serves at this juncture as a tangible reminder of the nature of Jamie's more immediate inheritance obligations. His payment of some of Beatrice's money to Kathleen, however, is in a sense the more fitting solution, for in effect he is using the money from one Mangan inheritance to cancel out the legacy from another.

The brief third and final section of the novel constitutes only an instant in Jamie's continuing quest for his identity, but in that moment the two things of import that he discovers—his father's imminent death and Margrethe's pregnancy—dramatize the two basic requirements of the very word "inheritance." Suddenly, therefore, Jamie senses the priority of his father's world over what he had discovered in Drishane:

Through his father—who knew nothing of Gorteen, Duntally, Norman towers, and lonely headlands—the uncanny facial resemblance, the poetry, the wild blood had been transferred across the Atlantic Ocean to this cold winter land, to this, his father's harsh native city in which he now lay dying. He looked at his father's face and wished that those features were his own. (*MI*, 336)

Though he cannot obliterate the past that he discovered in Ireland, his future, as the guardian of his father's child and perhaps as the husband of his widow (though I confess it is more my romantic impulse than Moore's evidence that evokes this prophecy), takes on a total authority. Just as Gavin in *The Emperor of Ice-Cream* found it necessary to obey the exigencies of the moment rather than the legacies of the past—and of course that novel closes, too, on a harmonious father-son resolution—so Jamie and Margrethe, one on either side of the dying man's bed, are compelled to sit and wait for the present and the future to blend into their new reality.

CHAPTER 7

Conclusion

THE fictional odyssey from *Judith Hearne* through the North American novels to *The Doctor's Wife* and *The Mangan Inheritance* not only parallels Moore's own exile and peregrinations, but, more importantly, it constitutes a remarkable and solid aesthetic achievement. In an age when many writers vie with media personalities for ephemeral public favor, Moore has gone quietly about the business of writing novels, and in the process has consolidated not only the beauty of fiction as an art form but also the relevance of fiction as a shaping component in our moral vision. In an extended essay covering Moore's fiction through *Catholics,* the critic DeWitt Henry elaborates perceptively on this point:

Moore's novels are designed to discover and exercise a widened sense of community in defiance of contemporary tendencies towards alienation, deracination, self-absorption, indifference to others, whether these are based on culturally conditioned values for glamour, or success, or sophistication, intellect, class, ethnic background, sex, or religion. The mode of that discovery is imaginative, ironic, and humanistic, and strenuously avoids . . . the easier and often rousing didactics that . . . essentially insulate and even congratulate the reader.[1]

Though Moore's novels on the whole are "easy" in the sense that on their narrative level they are readily accessible to the ordinary reader, they nevertheless reflect a disturbing world that poses both moral and existential dilemmas. His preoccupation with the loser, with the marginal character, with the individual at crisis, reflects both a sympathetic experiential observation of and involvement with ordinary people, and a subscribing to the possibilities of existential disaster: the center, indeed, may not hold, and through lack of choice, failure to choose, or paradoxically, making irrevocable choices, we run the risk of getting caught up in the moral chaos that could at any moment be let loose upon the world. Nevertheless,

150

as Moore's novels without exception assert, it is only within a moral and humanistic framework and through a strongly held personal commitment that fulfillment is at all possible, and this is a prescription Moore has consistently observed in his private life; unlike many of his characters, he has said, he is not afraid to gamble everything on a single toss.

Aesthetically, in spite of his occasional forays into fantasy, Moore is very much a traditional novelist whose greatest contribution to the state of contemporary fiction has been his reclamation of realism as a viable and flexible mode. It has allowed him to create a world of central and peripheral characters, in which he avoids the twin pitfalls of abstraction and caricature: the amoral and sluttish Kathleen Mangan, for example, is presented with as much compassion and understanding as the victimized Judith Hearne. Moore's realism is clearly in the tradition of the moral realism of a George Eliot or a Henry James and is reflected in our own literature by such writers as Margaret Laurence and Robertson Davies; not for him is the blunt, unfeeling realism of a James T. Farrell or a Hugh Garner, or the quasi-realistic caricature of a Charles Dickens or a Mordecai Richler.

Though he writes of the contemporary world, the spirit that informs his novels is in the fullest sense of the word a modern spirit, reflecting a vision which has its roots more in the metaphysical anguish of the nineteenth and early twentieth-century writers than in the ephemeral protests of the angry writers of Great Britain and North America. Nevertheless, as he pointed out to Donald Cameron, a writer must not disregard his obligations to his immediate world:

We, as writers, are losing sight of that real world in which our parents and relatives still live. In which the people in, say, Nova Scotia, or New Brunswick, or here in Toronto still live. Even ghetto people still live in a real, ordinary, dull world even though some of them pretend it's all Black Panther confrontations and heavy stuff, man. It's not true. Most people still live in the old-fashioned world of the nineteenth-century novels. . . . I'm terribly anxious to preserve those strong links with the real world. . . .[2]

It is "those strong links" which in a real sense not only have transformed his imagination and vision into powerful and tangible novels, but which also have connected him intimately with the ordinary reader for whom he has consistently chosen to write.

Moore has always evinced a mild surprise not only at the fact that academics have taken him up, but also at the various themes and symbolic meanings they purport to discover in his fiction. Like all living novelists, of course, Moore has the opportunity to modify any pronouncements on matters like these, and the critic who presumes to utter a final word prematurely runs the risk of being made to look silly by the author's very next book. The richness of Brian Moore's fiction to date, however, ensures the validity of a number of interpretations, and the prospect of novels yet to come renders relatively insignificant any temporary risk the critic might assume.

Notes and References

Preface

1. In a letter to the writer dated March 28, 1980, Moore briefly describes his new novel: "My new novel is set in London and is about Irish people on a week's holiday in London. It is realistic in technique and deals with protagonists rather like those in my early novels, but the time is the present. It is bleak and hard to categorise but I would say that it would fit most handily into [the] category: discoveries of self."

Chapter One

1. Hallvard Dahlie, "Brian Moore: An Interview," *Tamarack Review* 46 (Winter 1968): 23-24. This interview was conducted at Malibu, California, on June 12, 1967. Hereafter designated as "Interview."

2. Pronounced either "Bree-an" or "Bry-an."

3. Brian Moore, "The Expatriate Writer," *Antigonish Review* 17 (Spring 1974): 30.

4. Interview, p. 7.

5. Ibid., pp. 9-10.

6. Letter from Brian Moore to André Deutsch, June 12, 1954. *Brian Moore Collection*, University of Calgary Library, Special Collections Division. Hereafter cited as *Brian Moore Collection*.

7. Interview, pp. 15-16.

8. Letter from Brian Moore to André Deutsch, June 12, 1954. *Brian Moore Collection*.

9. Brian Moore, "The Writer as Exile," *Canadian Journal of Irish Studies* 2:2 (December 1976): 6.

10. D.A.N. Jones, "Brian Moore," *New Review* 2:19 (October 1975): 48.

11. Brian Moore, "Preliminary Pages for a Work of Revenge," *Midstream*, Winter 1961, p. 58.

12. Letter from Brian Moore to André Deutsch, June 12, 1954. *Brian Moore Collection*.

13. Rochelle Girson, "[Interview]," *Saturday Review*, October 13, 1962, p. 20.

14. Christopher Ricks, "The Simple Excellence of Brian Moore," *New Statesman*, February 18, 1966, p. 227.

Chapter Two

1. Joseph Hone, ed., *Irish Ghost Stories* (London, 1977), pp. 100-19.
2. Letter from Edward Weeks to Willis K. Wing, December 4, 1956. *Brian Moore Collection*.
3. "Bloody Ulster: An Irishman's Lament," *Atlantic*, September 1970, pp. 58-62.
4. "A Fresh Look at Montreal," *Holiday*, September 1959, pp. 50-55, 118, 120-21.
5. "The Week of the Great Hooley," *Holiday*, August 1969, pp. 26-29, 69-70.
6. "Get Thin Luxuriously Behind the Golden Door," *Nova*, May/June 1969, pp. 68-71.
7. *Canada*, by Brian Moore and the Editors of *Life* (New York, 1963).
8. "The People of Belfast," *Holiday*, February 1964, pp. 58-63.
9. The following book reviews are referred to in this section: "Double-Headed, Aquiline," *Spectator*, July 27, 1962, pp. 119-20 (Mary McCarthy's *On the Contrary*); "The Secret Behind Jenkins' Sneer," *Bookweek*, August 30, 1964, pp. 5, 13 (Anthony Powell's *The Valley of Bones*); "There's Life in the Old Novel House," *Book World*, November 26, 1972, p. 8 (Robertson Davies's *The Manticore*); "The Woman on Horseback," *Great Canadians: A Century of Achievement* (Toronto: The Canadian Centennial Publishing Company Ltd., 1965), pp. 96-98 (Gabrielle Roy's *The Tin Flute*); "The Albatross of Self," *Spectator*, May 4, 1962, p. 589 (Malcolm Lowry's *Hear Us O Lord From Heaven Thy Dwelling Place*); "The Eagle Was Like a Mother Hen," *Bookweek*, May 9, 1965, p. 4 (Edmund Wilson's *O Canada*); "Candide Redux," *National Observer*, November 2, 1974, p. 23 (Marie-Claire Blais's *St Lawrence Blues*); "Too Much Hocus in the Pocus," *Bookweek*, January 9, 1966, pp. 4, 12 (John Fowles's *The Magus*); "As the Proud White Swans Invade the Local Goose Pond," *Washington Post*, February 9, 1973, p. B5 (Clark Blaise's *A North American Education*); "The Crazy Boatloads," *Spectator*, September 29, 1961, p. 430 (Malcolm Cowley's *Exile's Return*).
10. Speech at Vancouver Public Library, Vancouver, B.C., November 26, 1962.
11. All quotations are from the original edition (Toronto, 1971). The pagination is identical in the American edition (New York, 1971).
12. Quoted in Ivor Davis, "The FLQ Goes to Hollywood," *Toronto Globe and Mail*, February 12, 1972.
13. Reported in a letter from Brian Moore to Michael Horniman, March 13, 1971. *Brian Moore Collection*.

14. Donald Cameron, "Brian Moore," *Conversations with Canadian Novelists*, 2 (Toronto, 1973), p. 72.

15. Albert Camus, *The Rebel* (New York: Vintage Books, 1956), 4.

16. Jeanne Flood, *Brian Moore* (Lewisburg, Penna., 1974), p. 89.

17. John Goode, "Stage Left," *Partisan Review* 39 (Spring 1972): 280.

18. Cameron, pp. 71-72.

Chapter Three

1. Robert Sullivan, "Brian Moore: A Clinging Climate," *London Magazine* 16:5 (December 1976/January 1977): 65-66.

2. All quotations are from the original edition (London, 1955). The pagination is identical in the Canadian edition (Toronto, 1955), the American edition (Boston, 1956), and the paperback Delta edition (New York, 1964).

3. John Wilson Foster, *Forces and Themes in Ulster Fiction* (Dublin, 1974), p. 151.

4. Details of the genesis and development of this story are in the *Brian Moore Collection*.

5. Letter from Brian Moore to André Deutsch, June 12, 1954. *Brian Moore Collection*.

6. Interview, p. 15.

7. Foster, p. 160.

8. George Eliot, *Adam Bede* (Boston: Houghton Mifflin Co.,1968), p. 151.

9. All quotations are from the original edition (Boston and Toronto, 1957).

10. Letter from Brian Moore to Mordecai Richler, January 3, 1958. *Brian Moore Collection*.

11. Letter from Brian Moore to Seymour Lawrence, September 21, 1956. *Brian Moore Collection*.

12. John A. O'Brien, ed., *The Vanishing Irish* (New York: McGraw-Hill Co., Inc., 1953).

13. Patrick B. Noonan, "Why Few Irish Marry," *The Vanishing Irish*, p. 45.

14. Sean O'Faolain, "Love Among the Irish," *The Vanishing Irish*, p. 120.

15. Interview, p. 18.

16. All quotations are from the original edition (Toronto, 1965). The pagination is identical in the American edition (New York, 1965).

17. Letter from Brian Moore to Diana Athill, February 10, 1957. *Brian Moore Collection*.

18. Malcolm Lowry, *Ultramarine* (Philadelphia and New York: J. B. Lippincott Co., 1962), p. 183.

19. Letter from Brian Moore to Rory Fitzpatrick, January 23, 1966. *Brian Moore Collection*.

Chapter Four

1. All quotations are from the original edition (Boston and Toronto, 1960).

2. James Hall, *The Tragic Comedians* (Bloomington: Indiana University Press, 1963), p. 5.

3. Cyrus Hoy, *The Hyacinth Room: An Investigation into the Nature of Comedy, Tragedy, and Tragicomedy* (New York: Alfred A. Knopf, 1964), p. 310.

4. Albert Camus, *The Myth of Sisyphus* (New York: Vintage Books, 1955), p. 9.

5. Cyrus Hoy, p. 312.

6. James Hall, p. 154.

7. Interview, p. 19.

8. "Robert Fulford Interviews Brian Moore," *Tamarack Review* 23 (Spring 1962): 14.

9. All quotations are from the original edition (Boston and Toronto, 1962).

10. David Watmough Interviews Brian Moore, CBC Radio, June 1, 1963.

11. Rochelle Girson, "[Interview]," *Saturday Review*, October 13, 1962, p. 20.

12. Ibid., p. 20.

13. *Brian Moore Collection*.

14. Granville Hicks, "Asphalt Is Bitter Soil," *Saturday Review*, October 13, 1962, pp. 20, 47.

15. Interview, pp. 19-20.

16. Robert Sullivan, "Brian Moore: A Clinging Climate," *London Magazine* 16:5 (December 1976/January 1977): 67.

17. Letter from Hugh MacLennan to Brian Moore, November 26, 1962. *Brian Moore Collection*.

18. All quotations are from the original edition (Toronto, 1970). The pagination is identical in the American edition (New York, 1970).

19. *Brian Moore Collection*.

20. Letter from Brian Moore to Michael Horniman, February 18, 1970. *Brian Moore Collection*.

Chapter Five

1. All quotations are from the Canadian edition (Toronto, 1972). The pagination is identical in the American edition (New York, 1973).

2. Interview with Brian Moore, CBC Radio, October 9, 1972.

3. *The Catholic Encyclopedia,* ed. Robert C. Broderick (Nashville and New York: Thomas Nelson Inc., Publishers, 1976), p. 598.

4. As reported in the *Sunday News,* November 25, 1973.

5. As reported in the *Calgary Herald,* April 8, 1980.

6. All quotations are from the original edition (Toronto, 1975). The pagination is identical in the American edition (New York, 1975).

7. Letter from Brian Moore to Jack McClelland, March 10, 1974. *Brian Moore Collection.*

8. Sullivan, p. 67.

9. Ibid., p. 69.

10. Letter from Brian Moore to Tom Maschler, November 20, 1975. *Brian Moore Collection.*

Chapter Six

1. All quotations are from the original edition (Toronto, 1968). The pagination is identical in the American edition (New York, 1968).

2. "Brian Moore Tells About *I Am Mary Dunne,*" *Literary Guild Magazine,* July 1968, p. 5.

3. Foster, p. 178.

4. All quotations are from the original edition (Toronto, 1976). The pagination is identical in the American edition (New York, 1976).

5. *Brian Moore Collection.*

6. "Patrick Hinon Interviews Brian Moore," CBC Radio, December 4, 1976.

7. Constance Beresford-Howe, *The Book of Eve* (Toronto: Macmillan, 1973), p. 9.

8. Doris Lessing, *The Summer Before the Dark* (London: Jonathan Cape, 1973), p. 153.

9. All quotations are from the original edition (Toronto, 1979). The pagination is identical in the American edition (New York, 1979).

Chapter Seven

1. DeWitt Henry, "The Novels of Brian Moore: A Retrospective," *Ploughshares* 2:2 (1974): 9.

2. Cameron, p. 75.

Selected Bibliography

The *Brian Moore Collection*, housed in the Special Collections Division of the University of Calgary Library, consists of fifty boxes of Moore material. Included are variant manuscript versions and published versions of his novels, short stories, screenplays, articles, and reviews; the manuscripts of an unpublished novel and of several unpublished stories; copious correspondence with agents, publishers, editors, critics, relatives, and friends; publishing contracts; a Commonplace Book and Working Diaries for the early years of his career At the moment, the *Brian Moore Collection* comprises materials relating to all his work through *The Great Victorian Collection*, as well as several manuscripts of *The Doctor's Wife*.

For a detailed listing of all writings by and about Moore up to 1975, the reader is referred to Richard Studing's thorough "Brian Moore Bibliography," *Éire-Ireland* 10 (1975): 89-105. Both Studing's bibliography and the one that follows omit the foreign-language editions of Moore's novels, a fairly complete set of which is housed in the Special Collections Division of the University of Calgary Library.

In my annotated list of secondary sources, I ignore the many excellent pieces which deal with only one novel and limit myself to those major articles which cover Moore's work in general.

PRIMARY SOURCES

1. Books (listed in chronological order)

Wreath for a Redhead. Toronto: Harlequin, 1951.
The Executioners. Toronto: Harlequin, 1951.
French for Murder. New York: Fawcett, 1954. Written under the pseudonym Bernard Mara.
A Bullet for My Lady. New York: Fawcett, 1955. Written under the pseudonym Bernard Mara.
Judith Hearne. London: André Deutsch, 1955. Toronto: Collins, 1955. Published from the same plates as *The Lonely Passion of Judith Hearne*. Boston and Toronto, 1956. Uniform Canadian edition: Toronto: McClelland and Stewart, Limited, n.d. Paperback editions: Dell, 1957; Penguin (as *The Lonely Passion of Miss Judith Hearne*), 1959; Delta, 1964; New Canadian Library, with Introduction by John Stedmond, 1964; Panther, 1965; Pocket Books, 1978.

This Gun for Gloria. New York: Fawcett, 1956. Written under the pseudonym Bernard Mara.

Intent to Kill. London: Eyre and Spottiswoode, 1956. Paperback edition: Dell, 1956. Written under the pseudonym Michael Bryan.

The Feast of Lupercal. Boston and Toronto: Atlantic-Little, Brown and Company, 1957. London: André Deutsch, 1958. Uniform Canadian edition: Toronto: McClelland and Stewart, Limited, n.d. Paperback editions: Panther (as *A Moment of Love*), 1965; Delta, 1965.

Murder In Majorca. New York: Dell, 1957. London: Eyre and Spottiswoode, 1958. Written under the pseudonym Michael Bryan.

The Luck of Ginger Coffey. Boston and Toronto: Atlantic-Little, Brown and Company, 1960. London: André Deutsch, 1960. London: Hutchinson Educational, 1966. Uniform Canadian edition: Toronto: McClelland and Stewart, Limited, n.d. Paperback editions: Dell, 1962; Penguin, 1965; New Canadian Library, with Intoduction by Keath Fraser, 1972; Quartet, 1973.

An Answer from Limbo. Boston and Toronto: Atlantic-Little, Brown and Company, 1962. London: André Deutsch, 1963. Uniform Canadian edition: Toronto: McClelland and Stewart, Limited, n.d. Paperback editions: Dell, 1963; Penguin, 1965; Paperjacks, 1973.

Canada. New York: Time, Inc., 1963. Written by Brian Moore and the Editors of *Life*.

The Emperor of Ice-Cream. Toronto: McClelland and Stewart, Limited, 1965; New York: The Viking Press, 1965; London: André Deutsch, 1966; Uniform Canadian edition: Toronto: McClelland and Stewart, Limited, n.d. Paperback editions: Bantam, 1966; Mayflower, 1967; Penguin, 1977.

I Am Mary Dunne. Toronto: McClelland and Stewart, Limited, 1968; New York: The Viking Press, 1968; London: Jonathan Cape, 1968; Paperback editions: Bantam, 1969; Penguin, 1973; New Canadian Library, with Introduction by Alan Kennedy, 1976.

Fergus. Toronto: McClelland and Stewart, Limited, 1970; New York: Holt, Rinehart and Winston, 1970. London: Jonathan Cape, 1971; Paperback edition: Penguin, 1977.

The Revolution Script. Toronto: McClelland and Stewart, Limited, 1971; New York: Holt, Rinehart and Winston, 1971; London: Jonathan Cape, 1972; Paperback edition: Pocket Book, 1972.

Catholics. New American Review, 15. New York: Simon and Schuster, 1972, pp. 11-72; Toronto: McClelland and Stewart, Limited, 1972; London: Jonathan Cape, 1972; New York: Holt, Rinehart and Winston, 1973; Paperback editions: Pocket Book, 1973; Penguin, 1977.

The Great Victorian Collection. Toronto: McClelland and Stewart, Limited, 1975; New York: Farrar, Straus and Giroux, 1975; London: Jonathan Cape, 1975; Paperback edition: Ballantine, 1976.

The Doctor's Wife. Toronto: McClelland and Stewart, Limited, 1976; New

York: Farrar, Straus and Giroux, 1976. London: Jonathan Cape, 1976.
Paperback editions: Bantam-Seal, 1977; Dell, 1977, Corgi, 1978.

Two Stories. Northridge, California: Santa Susana Press, 1978. Includes "Preliminary Pages for a Work of Revenge" and "Uncle T."

The Mangan Inheritance. Toronto: McClelland and Stewart, Limited, 1979; New York: Farrar, Straus and Giroux, 1979; London: Jonathan Cape, 1979. Paperback edition: Penguin, 1980.

The Temptations of Eileen Hughes. Toronto: McClelland and Stewart, Limited, 1981; New York: Farrar, Straus and Giroux, 1981.

2. Selected Short Stories (listed in chronological order)

"Sassenach," *Northern Review* 5 (October-November 1951): 2-8. Reprinted, with slight revisions, *Atlantic,* March 1957, pp. 47-49.

"A Vocation," *Tamarack Review* 1 (Autumn 1956): 18-22. Reprinted in *Threshold* 2 (Summer 1958): 21-25; *The Irish Genius,* ed. Devin A. Garrity. New York: Signet Books, 1960, pp. 125-28; *Threshold: An Anthology of Ulster Writing* 21 (Summer 1967): 49-53.

"Lion of the Afternoon." *Atlantic,* November 1957, pp. 78-83. Reprinted in *Cornhill* 170 (Autumn 1958): 149-58; *A Book of Canadian Stories,* ed. Desmond Pacey. Toronto: Ryerson, 1962, pp. 283-93.

"Next Thing Was Kansas City," *Atlantic,* February 1959, pp. 77-79.

"Grieve for the Dear Departed," *Atlantic,* August 1959, pp. 43-46. Reprinted in *Pick of Today's Short Stories, 12,* ed. John Pudney. London: Putnam, 1961, pp. 179-88.

"Uncle T," *Gentleman's Quarterly,* November 1960, pp. 118-19, 140, 142-54, 158. Reprinted in Brian Moore, *Two Stories.* Northridge: Santa Susana Press, 1978, pp. 23-58.

"Preliminary Pages for a Work of Revenge," *Midstream* 7 (Winter 1961): 57-61. Reprinted in *The Dolmen: Miscellany of Irish Writing,* eds. John Montague and Thomas Kinsella. Dublin: The Dolmen Press, 1962, pp. 1-7; in *Canadian Writing Today,* ed. Mordecai Richler. Penguin, 1970, pp. 139-45; in *Ploughshares* 2:2 (1974): 28-32; in Brian Moore, *Two Stories.* Northridge: Santa Susana Press, 1978, pp. 7-19.

"Hearts and Flowers," *Spectator,* November 24, 1961, pp. 743, 745.

"Off the Track," *Ten for Wednesday Night,* ed. Robert Weaver. Toronto: McClelland and Stewart, Limited, 1961, pp. 159-67. Reprinted in *Modern Canadian Stories,* eds. Giose Rimanelli and Roberto Ruberto. Toronto: The Ryerson Press, 1966, pp. 239-46.

"The Sight," *Irish Ghost Stories,* ed. Joseph Hone. London: Hamish Hamilton, 1977, pp. 100-19.

3. Selected Nonfiction (listed in chronological order)

"A Fresh Look at Montreal," *Holiday,* September 1959, pp. 50-55, 118, 120-21.

"Dining Out in Montreal," *Holiday*, August 1961, pp. 70-71, 75-80.

"The People of Belfast," *Holiday*, February 1964, pp. 58-63.

"Bloody Ulster: An Irishman's Lament," *Atlantic*, September 1970, pp. 58-62. Published also as "Now and Then," *Threshold* 23 (Summer 1970): 20-37.

"The Expatriate Writer," *Antigonish Review* 17 (Spring 1974): 27-30.

"The Writer as Exile," *Canadian Journal of Irish Studies* 2:2 (December 1976): 5-17.

SECONDARY SOURCES

1. Books

DAHLIE, HALLVARD. *Brian Moore*. Toronto: The Copp Clark Publishing Co., 1969. The first book on Moore, a biographical-critical introduction to his novels through *Mary Dunne*. Published as one of the Studies in Canadian Literature Series. Now out of print.

FLOOD, JEANNE. *Brian Moore*. Lewisburg, Penna.: Bucknell University Press, and London: Associated University Presses, 1974. A perceptive Freudian approach to Moore's novels through *Catholics*, but it perhaps works the father-son conflict too insistently, particularly evident in her interpretation of *The Revolution Script* as a novel to support this thesis. Published as one of the Irish Writers Series.

FOSTER, JOHN WILSON. *Forces and Themes in Ulster Fiction*. Dublin: Gill and Macmillan, 1974, esp. pp. 122-130, 151-185. A thorough and wide-ranging study of Ulster fiction, with generally very good sections on Moore's novels. I have reservations about Foster's somewhat Procrustean approach, which compels him to interpret Moore's novels undergoing a progression from a ritualized rural setting to a "dehumanised cosmopolis." Depends fairly consistently on von Gennep's *Rites of Passage* for his major thesis, but gives as well perceptive readings of Moore's novels through *Catholics*. An indispensable book for the background to Ulster fiction.

2. Interviews

BRAY, RICHARD T., ed. "A Conversation with Brian Moore." *Critic: A Catholic Review of Books and the Arts* 35 (Fall 1976): 42-48. A "Conference" type telephone discussion between University of Wisconsin students enrolled in a course entitled "The Catholic in Literature" and Mr. Moore. Moore defends both the importance of having a faith and his own personal decision to leave the Catholic Church.

CAMERON, DONALD. "Brian Moore." *Conversations with Canadian Novelists*, 2. Toronto: Macmillan of Canada, 1973, pp. 64-85. An excellent and wide-ranging interview in which Moore discusses his art and his works through *Catholics*. Expresses his strong views that *The Revolu-*

tion Script should not really be considered as one of his important books.

DAHLIE, HALLVARD. "Brian Moore: An Interview." *Tamarack Review* 46 (1968): 7-29. A transcript of an interview conducted at Malibu on June 12, 1967. Moore talks about the influence of his family and church on his writing career, and discusses his novels through *The Emperor of Ice-Cream*.

DE SANTANA, HUBERT. "Interview with Brian Moore." *Maclean's*, July 11, 1977, pp. 4-7. Moore discusses the issue of Quebec separatism and draws comparisons with the situation in Ireland; he sees a danger in what could ensue from misdirected nationalism. Also a brief discussion of *The Doctor's Wife* and influences on Moore's writing.

FULFORD, ROBERT. "Robert Fulford Interviews Brian Moore." *Tamarack Review* 23 (1962): 5-18. The earliest recorded interview, in which Moore discusses the early years of his career, his life in Canada, and his early novels. Important for his views on the approach he used in *Ginger Coffey*.

GRAHAM, JOHN. "Brian Moore." *The Writer's Voice*, ed. George Garrett. New York: Morrow Paperback Editions, 1973, pp. 51-74. Conducted just prior to the publication of *Fergus*, the genesis and nature of which Moore discusses quite thoroughly. Also some revealing comments on *Emperor, Mary Dunne*, and the impact made on Moore by Borges. One of the most useful of the existing interviews.

SALE, RICHARD B. "An Interview in London with Brian Moore." *Studies in the Novel* 1 (Spring 1969): 67-80. Conducted on July 13, 1967. Moore discusses the early influences on his career as a writer, and the processes he has undergone to become a more complex and experimental writer. A thorough and informative interview.

3. Articles

CRONIN, JOHN. "Ulster's Alarming Novels." *Éire-Ireland* 4 (Winter 1969): 27-34. A useful discussion of the novels of Michael McLaverty, Brian Moore, Forrest Reid, Janet McNeill, and Maurice Leitch. He sees Moore's three Belfast novels characterized by "a mordant savagery" directed toward Ulster's sectarian malaise. I disagree, however, with his conclusion that *Emperor* "is the most violent and embittered of them all."

DE SANTANO, HUBERT. "The Calligraphy of Pain." *Maclean's*, September 17, 1979, pp. 44-46. A sensitive portrait of Moore at his Malibu home, accompanying the writer's review of the just-published *Mangan Inheritance*. De Santano is wrong, I think, in his claim that Canadian critics have been reluctant to acknowledge Moore: Ludwig, Fulford, Beresford-Howe, and MacLennan were among our critics and writers to praise him in the early years of his career.

DORENKAMP, J. H. "Finishing the Day: Nature and Grace in Two Novels by Brian Moore." *Éire-Ireland* 13 (Spring 1978): 103-12. Argues persuasively that we really cannot understand *I Am Mary Dunne* or *Catholics* unless we are fully aware of how traditional Catholic beliefs and practices combine with contemporary elements to illustrate the workings of grace. Surprisingly, more convincing with *Mary Dunne* than with *Catholics*.

FOSTER, JOHN WILSON. "Crisis and Ritual in Brian Moore's Belfast Novels," *Éire-Ireland* 3 (Autumn 1968): 66-74.

————. "Passage Through Limbo: Brian Moore's North American Novels." *Critique: Studies in Modern Fiction* 13 (1971): 5-18. These two articles are incorporated, with modification, into Foster's book described in this bibliography, Secondary Sources, Section 1.

FRAYNE, JOHN P. "Brian Moore's Wandering Irishman—The Not-So-Wild Colonial Boy." *Modern Irish Literature: Essays in Honor of William York Tindall*, eds. Raymond J. Porter and James D. Brophy. New York: Twayne Publishers, Inc., 1972, pp. 215-34. An interesting analysis of Moore's novels through *Fergus*, though a bit heavy on plot summaries. He sees *Fergus* as Moore's "worst novel to date," and *Mary Dunne* as "a farewell to Canada," judgments which seem hastily taken. Frayne stresses Moore's relationship with Joyce, and his fixed attitude toward Ireland and his own Irish past.

FRENCH, PHILIP. "The Novels of Brian Moore." *London Magazine*, February 1966, pp. 86-91. A sympathetic reading of Moore's novels through *Emperor*.

GALLAGHER, MICHAEL PAUL. "The Novels of Brian Moore." *Studies* (Ireland) 60 (Summer 1971): 180-94. Sees Moore in the tradition of Henry James in that his fiction is concerned with the conjunction of two worlds of experience. A convincing reading of Moore as a "modern" novelist whose underlying vision is humanistic and personal. An excellent article.

HENRY, DEWITT. "The Novels of Brian Moore: A Retrospective." *Ploughshares* 2:2 (1974): 7-27. A passionately sympathetic account of Moore's works through *Catholics*, accompanied by a brief bibliography. Henry excites and provokes the reader into a thorough appreciation of Moore's talents; he sees Moore as a humanistic challenge to the contemporary prophets of alienation and indifference. All in all, an indispensable article.

KATTIM [*sic*], NAIM. "Brian Moore." *Canadian Literature* 18 (Autumn 1963): 30-39. Written in French, Kattan's article discusses the relationship of art and exile in Moore's novels through *Limbo*. Two serious mistakes: he attributes one speech to Brendan's mother which is in fact Jane's, and one to Devine which is Una's, both of which affect the conclusions he is drawing.

KERSNOWSKI, FRANK L. "Exit the Anti-Hero." *Critique: Studies in Modern Fiction* 10 (1967-68): 60-71. Covers Moore's novels through *Emperor;*

interesting for its prediction that Moore might well turn away from present events and write of the future and the past, as he subsequently did in *Catholics* and *The Mangan Inheritance*. Otherwise, a somewhat distorted interpretation of the nature of Moore's protagonists.

LUDWIG, JACK. "A Mirror of Moore." *Canadian Literature* 7 (Winter 1961): 18-23.

————. "Brian Moore: Ireland's Loss, Canada's Novelist." *Critique: Studies in Modern Fiction* (Spring-Summer 1962): 5-13. Pursues the Joycean influences touched upon in his earlier article, as well as the mirror imagery in Moore's novels. These articles are significant mainly to illustrate the early interest in Moore taken by a leading critic, and for their prediction that Moore would create "significant fictions undefined by national boundaries."

MCSWEENEY, KERRY. "Brian Moore: Past and Present." *Critical Quarterly* 18:2 (Summer 1976): 53-66. An intelligent account of Moore's fiction through *The Great Victorian Collection*, this article traces the links between Moore's early works and that later novel. Interprets the *Collection* in terms of fable and allegory in a tripartite relationship: the role of art, the creator's life, and the interplay of past and present. An indispensable article.

PROSKY, MURRAY. "The Crisis of Identity in the Novels of Brian Moore." *Éire-Ireland* 6 (Fall 1971): 106-18. In an account of Moore's novels through *Mary Dunne*, Prosky sees the twin forces of desire and guilt contributing to a crisis of identity in most of his protagonists. Social pressures compel them to fabricate dream worlds or visions as psychological defenses.

RICKS, CHRISTOPHER. "The Simple Excellence of Brian Moore." *New Statesman*, February 18, 1966, pp. 227-28. One of the earliest champions of Moore in England, Ricks sees as a major Moore contribution his "abolishing of brow-distinction" in fiction.

SCANLAN, JOHN A. "The Artist-in-Exile: Brian Moore's North American Novels." *Éire-Ireland* 12 (Summer 1977): 14-33. Title somewhat misleading in that almost half of the article is devoted to a non-North American novel, *Emperor of Ice-Cream*. Scanlan sees Gavin Burke as a kind of Stephen Dedalus figure anticipating the North American exiles.

STAINES, DAVID. "Observance without Belief," *Canadian Literature* 73 (Summer 1977): 8-24. A chronological examination of Moore's fiction from *Judith Hearne* through *The Doctor's Wife*, which stresses the conflicts between the demands of orthodox belief and the requirements of individual needs. Excessive plot summary and carelessness weaken this article, and it adds little that is new in Moore scholarship.

SULLIVAN, ROBERT. "Brian Moore: A Clinging Climate." *London Magazine* 16:5 (January 1976/December 1977): 63-71. Mainly about *The Doctor's Wife*, but the interview portion of the article allows Moore to give some important ideas about his earlier fiction, especially about his concept of Brendan Tierney, and his problems with *The Great Victorian Collection*.

WOODCOCK, GEORGE. "Rounding Giotto's Circle: Brian Moore's Poor Bitches." *Odysseus Ever Returning*. Toronto: New Canadian Library, 1970, pp. 40-49. Woodcock sees Moore as one of the few Canadian novelists capable, like the great Europeans, of creating powerful female characters, as evidenced in his depictions of Judith Hearne, Jane Tierney, and Mary Dunne.

Index